JAMES WOODSING

Grouse, Deer, and Uncle Willy

authorHOUSE®

AuthorHouse™
1663 Liberty Drive
Bloomington, IN 47403
www.authorhouse.com
Phone: 1-800-839-8640

This book is a work of non-fiction. Unless otherwise noted, the author and the publisher make no explicit guarantees as to the accuracy of the information contained in this book and in some cases, names of people and places have been altered to protect their privacy.

© 2009 James Woodsing. All rights reserved.

No part of this book may be reproduced, stored in a retrieval system, or transmitted by any means without the written permission of the author.

First published by AuthorHouse 8/27/2009

ISBN: 978-1-4490-0768-3 (sc)

Printed in the United States of America
Bloomington, Indiana

This book is printed on acid-free paper.

Cover Image: Jim and Uncle Willy are walking along an old logging road with the grouse Jim bagged with his single shot 22 rifle.

To Uncle Willy: *hunting companion, mentor, and friend.*

Acknowledgments:

Special thanks to Cory Fontaine for the cover picture and the beautiful illustrations. Thanks to friends and family for valuable input on the book and for the many conversations about hunting grouse and deer.

Table of Contents

Acknowledgments: vii
Chapter One   Learning to Shoot a Rifle 1
Chapter Two   Learning About Grouse and Hunting Grouse 11
Chapter Three   Uncle Willy Rescues His Brother Ned from a
                       Predicament 20
Chapter Four   Sparky and Wood Ticks. 27
Chapter Five   Grouse, Chimneys and a Cap Shoot 35
Chapter Six   The Hunting Camp 43
Chapter Seven   Compass Use: Who Made Those Tracks? 55
Chapter Eight   Practicing Survival 63
Chapter Nine   The Rifle 73
Chapter Ten   Uncles and Violating. 83
Chapter Eleven   My First and Second Bucks 90
Chapter Twelve   Musings in a Deer Blind 96
Chapter Thirteen   Counting Deer: Tracks after a Snow Fall 107
Chapter Fourteen   Trespassing. 114
Chapter Fifteen   Uncle Willy Reminisces 123

About the Author 133

Chapter One
Learning to Shoot a Rifle

Uncle Willy had taught me about fishing rods and brook trout fishing the previous two summers. Now that I was 12 years old, he thought it was time to introduce me to guns and hunting beginning on this Saturday afternoon in mid-September, 1949, on my grandparents' dairy farm. There was a lull in farm work as we had just harvested oats but were not quite ready to harvest potatoes. Grouse hunting season was rapidly approaching and would begin on Oct. 1. After three summers of great excitement catching brook trout, first with a government pole and then with a telescopic rod, Uncle Willy thought I was ready to begin hunting. He had introduced me to brook trout fishing as a nine year old so he must have thought three additional years of maturity were necessary before hunting.

After his service in the army infantry with a mortar unit in Europe during WWII, Uncle Willy stayed on the farm for several summers to my great advantage. Why? Because my father died in an automobile accident when I was just an infant and although I had five sisters, I had no brothers. To this day, with Uncle Willy now 92 yrs old, I am very appreciative that he assumed a father-figure role for me and taught me about fishing and hunting.

As we sat down for lunch, Uncle Willy said, "Jim buddy, after lunch, how about if you, cousin Jack, and I head out to the back of the farm for some target practice with the 22?" My mother, upon hearing this and knowing this would be my first time shooting any gun beyond my Daisy BB rifle, only said, "Be careful." My mother's main concerns about me at my young age were that I was healthy and happy and that I did my regular daily farm chores and contributed as best I could to seasonal farm work. My grandfather, on the other hand, mumbled something about me being too young to handle a rifle, as I was only 12, but Uncle Willy countered by saying that a youngster had to start sometime. It helped that Cousin Jack was visiting for an overnight, he being 2 years older than me. Jack had joined us brook trout fishing earlier in the summer and, like me, loved Uncle Willy. I was so excited I must have set a speed record for finishing lunch. My mother had to calm me down.

Uncle Willy instructed Jack and me to find some cardboard boxes, crayons, and some empty soup cans. He had us cut some small wooden stakes and sharpen the ends. He got his 22 Winchester down from a shelf in the closet and took three boxes of 22 cartridges out of a drawer. He draped an old, thick hunting coat over his arm, even though it was a warm day. When Uncle Willy mentioned zeroing-in the rifle, I immediately thought of Uncle Chuck, who would joke every fall prior to deer hunting season that he only needed two bullets, one to zero-in his rifle and one to shoot his deer. Uncle Chuck was drunk much of the time but at my age I thought that what I usually saw was his regular personality. In fact, without alcohol Uncle Chuck was a very quiet man and did not joke around at all.

We headed off to the back part of our 60 acre dairy farm, noted where the cows were grazing, and then headed a considerable distance from them. Uncle Willy pointed to the cows and asked us how far away we thought they were. Neither of us had an idea of their distance so he said, "they are about 200 yards from us right now but we want to be even farther away. A 22 rifle can carry 1 mile so they would be in our range anywhere on the farm; its the noise we want to minimize, to not upset them. Cows will give more milk if they are content and not upset."

We crossed Long Crick after taking a brief look under the bridge to see if a brook trout or two might be hanging in the current; one nice trout was present. Uncle Willy said, "In a few weeks trout will be breeding and we will see plenty of nice size brookies right out in the open, on their gravel nests, which are called redds." Uncle Willy had explained to me about trout breeding a couple of years earlier while we were fishing on Long Crick but he hadn't used that terminology, "trout sitting on a redd." I was curious at this time but did not ask, being a quiet kid and hardly saying more than two words in a day's time. But Uncle Willy was one of the few people I was comfortable talking to.

Reaching a hillside Uncle Willy surveyed the target practice area and we got started. We set up the stakes and leaned the cardboard against them with the dirt hillside behind. Then we made some 3 inch diameter targets on the cardboard with the crayons and we were almost ready for shooting. The direction of the shots was away from the cows and thus the bullets would go through the cardboard into the dirt of the hillside. Uncle Willy stepped off 25 yards from the target on reasonably level ground and marked that distance; then he stepped off an additional 25 yards and again marked that distance. That gave us both 25 and 50 yard shooting distances. We then walked back to the 25 yard position. Uncle Willy next showed us how to load the clip of his 22 with six cartridges and how to insert the clip from the underside of the rifle. He showed us 22 shorts, 22 long rifle, and 22 hollow point cartridges, noting that the hollow points were the most deadly for shooting game and could even kill a deer with a head shot. The shorts were the least accurate and least powerful but could be used for short range shooting of mice, chipmunks, or squirrels..

Then Uncle Willy showed us the rifle's sights and explained that this rifle had "open" sights; he then explained how to sight the rifle on the target. Next he gave us a lesson on handling a rifle. "Always assume a rifle is loaded," he said, "and thus keep the barrel pointed toward the ground or up toward the sky. Never point a rifle at a person or non-game animal or in the direction of a farm or house or car or truck. When a cartridge is in the chamber, be sure the rifle is on safety. The person with the rifle should be in front, others in back." He showed us how the safety worked. Then he pulled the bolt open and we watched a cartridge get pushed into the chamber. He then reminded us about the safety and showed us that the safety was on. These safety rules were re-enforced into us on many occasions by Uncle Willy in such a way as to never seem like he was "preaching" to us.

At this point Uncle Willy rolled up the old hunting coat he had brought along and placed it on the ground. Then he laid down on his belly and with his elbows on the ground, placed the rifle on the old coat. He explained that the coat had just enough "give" but yet was firm enough to make sighting the rifle to the target very steady. He again explained how he was doing the sighting; his left eye was closed and he looked down the barrel of the rifle with his open right eye. The bead of the front sight would be sitting in the very bottom of the V of the back sight, but "you have to see the entire bead but no more," he explained. The bead was then placed in the center of the target of choice, his being the upper left target. "When I fire," he said, "I try to pull the trigger back without jerking, it's called squeezing the trigger, and I try not to blink my right eye. If you blink or jerk that is called a flinch." Uncle Willy was very deliberate, showing no sign of wanting to rush. I was standing there fidgeting, anxious to see some shooting. Even when brook trout fishing, I would be anxious to try the next hole without thoroughly fishing the hole I was at. Uncle Willy then clicked off the safety, aimed, and fired. He pulled the bolt back and ejected the empty shell and pushed another cartridge into the chamber. He fired 6 times at the upper left target, emptying the clip. Then he left the bolt open, laid the rifle down, and we all walked to the target. He explained that the sights should not need much adjustment as the rifle was shooting very accurately the previous year and no one had used it since to his knowledge. Sure enough, 5 of the shots were in the red bull's-eye and the 6th was just off the edge of the red circle. "Ahh," he said, "I must have flinched on this one," as he pointed to the one shot outside of the bull's-eye.

"OK boys, let's see how you do," he said, and we walked back to the 25 yard position. He had Jack go first. Jack had to load the clip, put it into the rifle, check that the safety was on, push a cartridge into the chamber by opening and closing the bolt, get down on his belly and elbows, and take aim. Uncle Willy asked, "do you understand how to sight the rifle to the target? Aim at the upper right target. OK, if you are ready, take the safety off and go ahead and fire once." A 22 has very little if any "kick back," there being only a small amount of powder in a cartridge, but it has a characteristic "crack" when it is shot, which is not very loud but very distinct. I was watching the target and heard the crack of the shot. Uncle Willy was watching Jack and said, "Jack, you flinched pretty badly on that shot."

Cousin Jack flinches. *Cousin Jack takes a shot while lying down with the 22 rifle steadily braced on the old coat bundled up on the ground. Uncle Willy and Jim are seated next to him looking toward the target. Uncle Willy can see from the corner of his eye that Jack flinched, causing him to miss far to the right of the bull's-eye.*

"Go ahead and take another shot." After the second shot, Uncle Willy again told Jack that he had flinched. I had watched Jack that time and did see that his right eye closed when he shot. Uncle Willy decided we would look at the target after those two shots. Jack had missed several inches to the right of the bull's-eye and his two shots had just barely stayed on the cardboard. Uncle Willy suggested that his flinch caused a slight pull of the trigger and the rifle to the right, sending the bullet off target. He further noted that being that far off would result in missing a grouse entirely or possibly hitting a deer with a deer rifle but not with a killing shot. Jack shot 10 more times with us checking the target after five and then after 5 more. His proficiency improved greatly and of his last 5 shots, 3 were in the bull's-eye. Uncle Willy kept reminding him to stay calm, to squeeze the trigger, and to not flinch.

Finally it was my turn. I had the benefit of listening to Uncle Willy's instructions to Jack plus his repeating the instructions for me. What Uncle Willy did not know was that I had practiced not flinching while Jack was shooting and I knew that during his last 5 shots I did not flinch. Sure enough, when I fired, I did not flinch except maybe two times and Uncle Willy did not say anything. Those two shots were probably two of the three that were outside the bull's-eye. My other 7 shots were within the bull's-eye. All Uncle Willy said was, "you would have killed a grouse just about every time."

Uncle Willy then said, "well, let's see if we can kill a grouse from 50 yards." Doubling the distance was a lot more challenging. The target looked considerably smaller and the sights larger in relation to the target. Furthermore, the shake of the rifle barrel, even on the bundled up coat, was more noticeable. Still, Uncle Willy hit the bull's-eye most of the time and both Jack and I hit it at least some of the time.

We weren't finished yet. Uncle Willy said, "Now we have to shoot under more realistic hunting conditions. We can't carry this old coat along when hunting and we aren't going to lie down on our belly either. We will most often have to shoot standing up and not even have anything to hold the rifle against, like a tree trunk or branch, to steady it. So, let's try free-standing shots. I'll go first." We set up a new piece of cardboard with 3 bull's-eyes in red. Uncle Willy decided we would shoot from only 50 yards. He explained that to shoot standing up one had to brace the legs, take a deep breath and hold it, and try to be as steady as possible. I watched him carefully and tried to learn. His shots all hit the cardboard near the bull's-eye or were within the bull's-eye. Jack did not hit the bull's-eye even once and he missed the cardboard some of the time. I immediately felt the weight of that 22, but surprisingly held it steady and avoided flinching. I hit the bull's-eye twice and was close all the other times. We then placed an empty soup can upside down on each of 3 stakes and we took turns shooting at the cans, with each of us taking 5 shots. That was fun as we could see the can get jolted if we hit it. Uncle Willy's can had 5 holes in it, Jack's had two, and mine had three.

"We did some pretty good shooting, boys," said Uncle Willy, without comparing any of us, and added, "Next time we practice we will get even better and by grouse season we will all be ready." Uncle Willy had a way of making us seem like a team. He did the same while trout fishing. Even if he caught all the trout, when we got home he would say, "We did alright. We caught a few but some big ones got away from us."

Finally, Uncle Willy showed us how to adjust the sights if the rifle was not shooting accurately. It was the back sight that would be adjusted, up, down, left or right, and usually only a very slight adjustment would be necessary. In the case of his 22 rifle that day, there was no need for any adjustments, as he had predicted before we began the target shooting.

We picked up all the empty cartridges we could find, took down the target, pulled up the stakes, gathered up the soup cans, and headed back to the farm. This time there were two nice sized brook trout under the bridge over Long Crick, drifting lazily in the current, causing Uncle Willy to remind us that trout fishing season was open until the last Saturday of the month. Then he said, "Jack and Jim, we should fish the spring hole on Black Crick one more time before the season closes." I must have been the happiest kid in that entire farming community. It wasn't until years later that I realized how fortunate I was to have Uncle Willy as a fishing and hunting companion and mentor. He was special! That evening, before going to bed, I pretended having a rifle and aiming it at a grouse or deer. I'd say "bang" and then visualize the grouse or deer toppling over. I never flinched and never missed.

Speaking about flinching, David E. Petzal had an article in Field and Stream magazine (2008) titled: "Cure The Flinch." He stated that the flinch is mainly caused by anticipating the recoil (kick back) of the rifle and that "a flinch is likely caused by the body's very sensible reaction to the knowledge that something awful is about to happen to it." His 4 cures for the flinch were: 1. Admit you have a problem and work at solving it. 2. Go to a smaller gun. 3. Get a Caldwell Lead Sled (secure your rifle to this sled and it will not do damage to your shoulder). 4. Shoot more, not less. Fortunately, Jack and I solved our flinching with steps 1, 2, and 4, and with the encouragement from Uncle Willy, and did not have to resort to the lead sled. It was best we began with a 22 which had no noticeable kick-back.

Chapter Two
Learning About Grouse and Hunting Grouse

Before I ever saw a ruffed grouse, I heard one. It was the male "drumming" and the sound was called to my attention by Uncle Willy while we were brook trout fishing on Long Crick on our dairy farm in early May. I was 9 years old and still remember that day and how fascinating that drumming sound was. Uncle Willy had stopped us and said, "listen," and we stood still for several minutes while we listened to repeated drummings. He then explained that the drumming sound is the result of the male grouse beating the air with its wings against its chest, starting slowly, boom......... boom..........boom and then speeding up until the beats are very close together, boom,boom,boom, and very fast. Its a very unique sound! If someone heard that sound and did not know it was a grouse drumming, I wonder what that person might think it was. Catching brook trout and hearing grouse drumming are two of life's small pleasures that I experienced on the same spring day.

The scientific name of the American ruffed grouse is *Bonasa umbellus*; it is one of a group of 16 grouse species, the closest being the hazel grouse of Eurasia and China. The American ruffed grouse, often referred to as a partridge or pat, is the only species wherein the male calls for its mate by drumming; it does this when standing on a fallen tree, the so-called "drumming log." It is very difficult to sneak up on a drumming grouse as these males are very wary. I have tried more than once only to find that the drumming stops before I get close enough to see the drumming male.

In addition to the drumming behavior by the male, the ruffed grouse has the characteristic "ruff" around the neck, a tail that fans out, distinctive tail bands, and feathered legs. During our first few hunting trips Uncle Willy told me that grouse will often stay on the forest floor, either standing still, slowly or quickly walking, or sometimes running, and thus the hunter may not see the bird. Grouse have visited my bait pile during deer hunting season many times and seldom does one "fly" in. They most often walk in and, after feeding, walk out again. When a grouse does take flight, i.e. when it flushes, there is again an unmistakable sound, best imitated by blowing air through one's pursed lips. The flushed grouse can often be heard without being seen. The size of grouse populations can be estimated by counting drumming birds in the spring time or by counting flushes in the autumn.

Most of what I learned about grouse was initially taught to me by Uncle Willy, later by my Cousin Ric, then gained via my own experiences out in the woods, and decades later from the wonderful book, "The Wildlife Series, Ruffed Grouse," Edited by Sally Atwater and Judith Schnell, Stackpole Books, 1989.

The ruffed grouse has always been my favorite bird. Occasionally someone will ask me how I can hunt grouse if it's my favorite bird. My answer is that I bag very few each season and that my concern is to preserve the species, not necessarily an individual bird. Then I point out a well-known fact which is that if humans want to make sure an animal or bird does not become extinct, make it a game animal or game bird and open a hunting season for it. Hunters will work very hard to insure that there is good habitat for that species and that hunting is regulated so that that game animal/bird can be enjoyed for many decades.

Uncle Willy taught me to recognize good grouse habitat, the best being stands of young big-tooth aspen (poplar or popple) with interspersed evergreens. He said that white birch and various berry and seed-producing trees and shrubs were also good, but mature forests with little light reaching the forest floor would seldom have grouse. Grouse liked to hang around thickets, berry patches, stream bottoms, and along old logging roads that had white clover growing on them and with exposed gravel. It was to these kinds of habitats that Uncle Willy took me to hunt.

Uncle Willy bought me a used single shot 22 rifle for my 13th birthday and that summer we zeroed it in at both 25 and 50 yards. Having learned not to flinch, I got so I could hit the bull's-eye from a resting position most of the time, less often but still at a high percentage with a free-standing shot, i.e. without resting the rifle on a tree branch or stump to steady it. My nerves were good as a youth. Uncle Willy was in his mid-30s and was a better shot than me. That was the rifle I carried this first time Uncle Willy took me grouse hunting. He impressed upon me that with my 22 I should only shoot at a grouse on the ground and that hitting a flying grouse with a 22 was near impossible. Finally, he reminded me that a 22 has a 1 mile range so it should only be fired towards the ground. He carried a 20 gauge (GA) pump action shotgun. He had already shown me how to shoot this 20 GA and had explained shotguns in general and their ammunition (fine-shot, buck-shot, and slugs) and the game for each, including pointing out that at one time 4 GA and 10 GA shotguns were manufactured but presently the 12 GA was the most powerful. The killing power decreased as the GA increased: 12, 16, 28, and 410. Uncle Willy even owned a single shot 410 GA pistol, with a barrel about 15 inches long, and we occasionally shot that odd pistol behind the barn. The BBs would spread very quickly so it was really worthless for hunting but still a fascinating firearm.

There was considerable logging going on during my youth, the late 40's into the 50's, and the usual practice was for a logging company to "clear cut" everything, leaving only stumps and thus no game animal habitat. But within a few years raspberries, blackberries, and other shrubs would grow in. I remember picking raspberries with my sisters, our mother, and one or more uncles and cousins during the peak berry season. Those fresh raspberry pies were delicious and canned berries on hot rice in the winter was a special treat. We would pick strawberries in June, raspberries in July, and blueberries and blackberries in August. Berry picking was a necessary activity on the farm. Thinking back, it seems that in this small farming community we probably obtained much of our vitamin C, not to mention anti-oxidants, from canned berries during the winter. We could rarely afford fresh fruit.

While the raspberries were spreading through the clear-cut areas, aspen began to grow in and when the saplings reached 10-20 feet high, the area was called a "slashing." It was tough going directly through slashings so old logging roads were the choice. Ideally a hunter would have a cocker spaniel, the dog of choice for grouse hunting at that time, to flush the grouse from the thickets of aspen and evergreens along the sides of the old logging roads. Uncle Willy and I seldom hunted with a dog but we bagged our share of grouse nevertheless.

This quiet Saturday morning in early October, Uncle Willy and I were deliberately making our way along an old logging road that was becoming overgrown with brush from the sides. I was always anxious to get over the next hill or around the next curve and Uncle Willy had to slow me down. There were open areas and white clover was growing here and there. Occasional spots of gravel were also present. Uncle Willy called my attention to grouse "poop" within a patch of clover; it looked somewhat like chicken poop but had more color to it. He explained to me that grouse will fill their crop with clover and then eat some gravel to help their gizzard grind up the clover for easier digestion. I didn't really have a feeling for either a crop or a gizzard but he offered no more explanation.

All of sudden we heard the unmistakable flush sound of a grouse. Uncle Willy, walking ahead of me, raised his shotgun but we only caught a fleeting glimpse of the bird. "I wasn't ready," he said. Then added, "you have to really be alert to bag a grouse." I learned that principle early on. It always seems to me that 98 percent of the time a grouse flushes when you least expect it. Often one only hears it. We continued walking slowly along the old road. After rounding a bend, Uncle Willy stopped and called my attention to an object about 40 yards ahead of us sitting in the clover in the middle of the old road. "That could be a partridge," he whispered. We both studied the object and after a short time Uncle Willy thought it might be just a piece of wood. Anyway, he decided it might be an opportunity for me to fire a shot with my 22 and if it was not a partridge, there would be no harm done. "If its a partridge and you miss, I might have a shot with my 20 GA," he added. So, with Uncle Willy on my right side about 6 feet away, ready with his shotgun, I pulled the hammer back on my 22, took aim, and fired. The object crumpled and almost disappeared into the clover. We walked up and, sure enough, it was a grouse and I had hit it in the middle of the chest, right through the breastbone. "Pretty good shot," said Uncle Willy. That was the only grouse we bagged that day although we flushed several more. Uncle Willy did shoot at one but it flushed into a thicket and it was a difficult chance. I had the time of my young hunting life.

GROUSE, DEER, AND UNCLE WILLY

Jim's first grouse. *Jim and Uncle Willy are walking along an old logging road that has clover growing on it. Jim is happily carrying a grouse which he bagged with one shot from his 22 single shot rifle from 40 yards. Uncle Willy is proud of his nephew's shooting ability. They are heading back to the car, already thinking about grouse for dinner.*

When we got home we took the grouse behind the barn and Uncle Willy first showed me its crop, a sack underneath the neck. The crop was full of clover and Uncle Willy said, "We know what this grouse was doing in the middle of that logging road; it was eating clover." Then Uncle Willy showed me how to pull the skin and feathers off together. This was unlike the case with chickens, which are doused in boiling water and the feathers are "plucked," leaving the skin on. Then he showed me how to lift the breastbone and expose the innards, or "guts," as he called them. He didn't identify the individual organs as he did with brook trout, but he did point out the gizzard, the grinding organ. The guts came out easily leaving the clean, sort of grayish colored breasts and the dark hind legs. There wasn't much meat on one grouse but it was very good; we had fried grouse that evening for dinner and everyone had a taste.

Uncle Willy told my mother and grandparents that I had bagged that grouse with a free-standing shot from quite a long way away. My grandmother gave my hair a tussle. My grandfather said I would be shooting many more. My mother smiled at me but didn't say anything. She knew I was happy doing things with Uncle Willy, especially brook trout fishing, and now she realized we had another activity to do together, grouse hunting. I was so excited I could hardly get to sleep that night, rethinking everything about that day.

I still relish grouse once or twice in October if I'm lucky enough to bag one. What a treat! And I still get excited about grouse hunting. No two days of hunting are ever the same. Last fall I was hunting with my buddy Ted who has a great hunting dog, a springer spaniel. We were walking down an old two-track, me in front. Ted had left his shotgun in his van, deciding to just enjoy the fall day while working his dog. After about 15 minutes of walking through great grouse country, we rounded a corner and the dog flushed a grouse which headed down the two track. I lifted my shotgun for a perfect shot but I couldn't shoot. The grouse was flying only 4 feet off the ground, right down the two track, but right in line with a doe that was standing in the middle of that old logging road looking at us, about 75 yards away. If I had fired, some of those BBs would have hit the doe. That grouse flew right over that deer's back, kept going until it was out of range, and then veered into a thicket. Ted and I shook our heads and laughed. It was as if that grouse knew we wouldn't shoot with the deer on the road.

Chapter Three
Uncle Willy Rescues
His Brother Ned from a Predicament

It was October, the maples were in full color, and Uncle Willy and Aunt Tess had taken vacation time from their California jobs and returned home to the farm, mainly so Uncle Willy could go hunting. One of the first things Uncle Willy did was to visit his brother Ned and arrange to go "bird" (pat/partridge/grouse) hunting. They arranged to meet early the next morning as Ned was always happy to get out hunting with Willy. Ned was not much of a grouse hunter but he liked the idea of getting out into the woods in case "something bigger" showed up. The "something bigger" was referring to a bear or a deer. Both Uncle Willy and Ned had a bear permit but deer hunting was not legal until mid-November. Thus, to be ready for bigger game, both men took along a pocket full of shotgun slugs for big game in addition to fine-shot for small game. Uncle Willy carried a pump action 20 GA shotgun while Ned carried a single shot 20 GA. Ned shouldered a pack sack into which he added some sandwiches, a thermos of coffee, and a hatchet.

A stray dog, a beagle, happened into Ned's yard just as they were getting ready to head into the woods so the two men decided to take the dog along, thinking it might scare up a rabbit or flush a grouse. The two men, after a biscuit and coffee, and the dog, after a small piece of biscuit and some water, set off into the forest. It was going to be a warm October day, over 40 degrees. After an hour or so of walking slowly together, the dog having flushed two grouse but neither bird close enough to shoot at, Uncle Ned suggested he sit for awhile (posting as it was called) to watch for any kind of game, and he kept the dog with him. Uncle Willy set off over a small ridge through maples and some evergreens.

No sooner had Uncle Willy ventured off, about one eighth mile or so, he came upon 2 black bears eating choke cherries from the ground under a choke cherry tree. He immediately opened his 20 GA and replaced the fine-shot shell with a slug. This noise and activity startled the bears somewhat. He raised his shotgun and fired at the bear that was closest to him but it was a long shot and he missed. Before he could re-load with another slug, that bear ran toward the other one and together the 2 bears ran in Ned's direction. After a few moments, a shot resounded and that was followed by a huge ruckus, with screaming and dog barking, from the vicinity where Ned presumably was posting. Uncle Willy asked himself whether his brother might have gotten into trouble as the bears had headed directly for him. The ruckus did not decrease so Uncle Willy headed towards where he had left his brother. About half way there another shot rang out.

When Uncle Willy got there, he was relieved that his brother was fine and he could see one dead bear lying under a cluster of cherry trees. Both Ned and the barking dog were looking up into the cluster of trees. Ned calmly exclaimed that the 2 bears came right toward him and the dog stopped them just long enough so that he could shoot the larger one, now only 20 feet away. The dog then chased the smaller bear up the largest of the cherry trees. Ned subsequently shot the smaller bear which appeared to be dead but it was lodged firmly in the crotch of the tree, about 25 feet up. My guess is that Uncle Ned already had a slug in his shotgun so he was ready when those bears came in his direction. The men reasoned that the smaller bear stuck up in the tree was the female and the dead bear on the ground was the male. So the question was what to do about the bear lodged up in the tree.

"I'll climb up and dislodge it," said Uncle Willy, and he put his shotgun down and proceeded to climb by circling his arms and legs around the trunk and shimming himself upwards. At about 12 feet above ground, still another 12 feet from the bear, he stopped, looked down, and said to Ned, "I'm not a kid anymore; I'm so out of shape I can't make it any further. My heart is pounding so hard I'm coming down." He was completely winded. Ned then said, "OK, let me try it." Well, Ned didn't even get to 12 feet and gave up. But, as he lowered himself down, one leg got caught between two of the trees in the clump. He was so tired he could not get back up high enough to free that leg and both men realized the predicament Ned was in. Uncle Willy encouraged Ned to climb back up aways and lift that leg up but Ned could not. If Ned had let loose, the leg would have been fractured or, at the minimum, Ned would have been left hanging from one leg. Ned's breathing was so labored by now that Uncle Willy thought he might have a heart attack. Quickly evaluating the situation and knowing there wasn't much time before his brother would have to let go from exhaustion, Uncle Willy pulled a dead log over and set it under Ned. Then he said to Ned, "On the count of three, I'm going to push you up. You pull up as hard as you can and at the same time lift your leg out." While standing precariously on the log, Uncle Willy counted, "one, two, THREE" and pushed upward on his brother's backside. After a moment, Ned's leg came swinging down and banged into Uncle Willy's rib cage, and at the same time Ned lost his grip on the tree and the two of them spilled onto the forest floor, about a foot from the dead bear. Both were relieved that neither was injured.

Uncle Ned is rescued by Uncle Willy. *In an attempt to dislodge the dead bear that is caught up in a choke cherry tree, Uncle Ned tried to climb up the tree but couldn't make it high enough. On the way down his foot got caught between two of the tree trunks and he had to be boosted up by Uncle Willy to free his stuck leg. The other bear lies dead on the ground. The stray dog is watching the events.*

They brushed themselves off and chuckled at each other. They likely had had plenty of these kinds of adventures as youths growing up on the farm. Uncle Willy asked, "How did you get your foot caught like that?" Ned replied, "I guess I was so tired I didn't realize my leg went between those two trees while coming down." Quite exhausted, they each ate a sandwich and had a drink of lukewarm coffee that Ned produced from his pack sack. After the snack, they cooperated again and field-dressed the larger bear, which was a male, then pulled it over a log so that the blood would drain from its body cavity. By now it was late afternoon and both men were very tired so they left the bears there, one still in the tree, and headed home. Then Ned added, "We will get that bear down in the morning." It was fortunate the night got very cold which helped preserve the bear's meat.

The next morning, now each with a pack sack, they returned to the same spot and Ned produced a hatchet from his pack sack." Nowadays we call it a backpack. Yes, it was a hatchet "but a very dull one," Uncle Willy recalled when retelling this story. Nevertheless, both men took turns and finally got that choke cherry tree cut through, and recovered the dead bear, a female. They then skinned both bears, cut off the choice pieces of the meat, mainly the back and hind quarters, and loaded one pack sack with meat and the other with the skin from the male bear. Ned was going to process and "tan" that bear hide for his living room wall. When they got home, word had gotten around that they had bagged two bears and their cousin Jake came by asking if he could have some of the meat "Sure," they both said, and Uncle Willy agreed to lead him to the spot the following day. After two days of temperatures in the

40's and part of a 3rd day, flies had already been attracted to the exposed meat and some of it apparently began to emit an unpleasant odor. Uncle Willy didn't think it was warm enough for meat to spoil in that short a time but he said bear meat typically has an unpleasant odor anyway. Whatever it was, something turned Jake's stomach and he had to go over behind a nearby tree and puke. Even so, when he recovered somewhat, the two men cut off what was left of the healthiest of the meat and packed it home. Uncle Willy could not recall if Jake's family actually ate any of it and whether or not they enjoyed it.

Some of the meat was canned by a neighbor lady and Uncle Willy recalled taking it back to Calif. It was "very good" he told me. Ned did not get around to immediately processing that hide and soon there was a noticeable foul odor coming from the barn that his wife, with a look of disgust, called to his attention. Sure enough, the hide had spoiled and it had to be thrown out.

That 3 day period had such an impact on Uncle Willy that even now, at 92 years of age, he can still remember it in great detail.

Chapter Four
Sparky and Wood Ticks.

The year I was in 7th grade, my cousin Ric, who was in 10th grade, obtained a brown and white cocker spaniel puppy that was so full of energy he gave it the name Sparky. His older sister and my older sister did summer work at a resort in N. Wisconsin and a fellow they knew there offered the puppy to Ric. That puppy grew quickly through the fall and winter and was full-grown by the following summer. I have to point out here that mid-summer was the peak time for wood ticks. Ric was looking forward to grouse hunting with Sparky that coming October but the dog had to be trained. As often as possible, Ric would take Sparky out into the woods, trying to simulate grouse hunting.

One rather warm day he asked me if I wanted to join him to see how Sparky was progressing in the training and of course I said yes. About 9 AM, we headed into some ideal grouse habitat at the back of their farm, an area with mostly young aspen but also with evergreens, maples and birches scattered in. Ric did not take a rifle or shotgun and instead he carried an old gunny (feed) sack that was tied with a cord around the end. I wondered about the contents of the sack. When we were ready, he opened the gunny sack to show me the contents. Inside were feathers, bones, pieces of skin and a few heads, all belonging to grouse he had bagged the previous fall. "Go ahead, smell it," Ric said. Everything was very dry inside the sack and I could not detect odor of any kind, certainly not of rotting flesh. Of course back then we had no freezers so it was not possible to preserve an entire grouse through that many months.

Ric had me hold Sparky on his leash and he then set off through the aspen, evergreens, and shrubs dragging that gunny sack containing grouse parts behind him. After about 10 minutes of thrashing through the woods, during which time I could either see him or hear him, he returned without the gunny sack. Ric's strategy was to leave grouse scent around trees, over logs, under logs, over stumps, and in the brush, and then hang the bag from a branch just out of the reach of Sparky. Ric explained to me that these cocker spaniels, and of course most dogs, had a sense of smell probably thousands of times better than that of humans, consistent with their wolf ancestry. Biologists now know that dogs have many, many times more odor receptors in their nose than humans, accounting for their keen sense of smell. The idea was that various grouse odor molecules would escape through the gunny sac, it not being air-proof as today's plastic bags might be, and Sparky could detect these molecules.

GROUSE, DEER, AND UNCLE WILLY

Cousin Ric and Jim are training Sparky, a grouse hunting cocker spaniel. *While Jim holds Sparky, Cousin Ric runs through the woods over stumps and dead trees pulling the gunny sack with grouse parts in it. Ric then ties the gunny sack in a tree and Jim releases Sparky to follow the scent to the "grouse."*

"OK, let's let Sparky loose and see if he can follow that trail," Ric said. He opened the snap to Sparky's leash, started him on the gunny sack trail, and encouraged him by saying, "Go Sparky, get that partridge. Go Boy!" Sparky kept his nose to the ground and headed through the brush and poplars. Every so often Ric would yell out, "Go Sparky, find that partridge," as the two of us chased after him. Sparky would occasionally let out a bark or yelp as he followed the trail made by the gunny sack. Then, all of sudden, Sparky began to bark in earnest and I wondered what he was barking at. "He has flushed a partridge and its in a tree," explained Ric, as we ran toward Sparky. Well, not exactly, I noted, but he was jumping up and down under the gunny sack hanging from the tree limb, barking like crazy. In the dog's mind, that sack was a partridge. "Good boy, Sparky," Ric said to his dog and scratched his ears and gave him a small treat of dried meat.

We repeated this scenario several times, trying to find somewhat different kinds of habitat. Ric let me drag the gunny sack a couple of times. Sparky located the sack and "treed the partridge" every time. Now it was getting near lunch and time to head back for farm chores. While walking back home, more than once Ric and I detected a wood tick crawling up the back of our neck and we grabbed it between our forefinger and thumb. Then with finger and thumb nail, we would split off its head and discard the parts. Such a procedure was commonplace on our farms after a period of time in the woods.

When we arrived in Ric's yard, about a 20 minute walk from where we did the sack dragging, Ric said, "before you go home, let's see if Sparky has any wood ticks." Our farm was about a quarter mile up the road. Ric found an old coffee can and poured about a half inch of gasoline into it. He knew there would be more than a few wood ticks on that dog, but neither of us had an idea how many.

There were so many wood ticks on that dog, it was truly amazing. Some were already attached and gorged with blood and undoubtedly had been on Sparky for a day or more. The largest of the gorged wood ticks were approximately a third of an inch long and quarter of an inch in diameter, gray in color. They were ugly; gross would be the modern word to describe them. Every size in between was found, including many ticks that were not yet attached. As we pulled them off Sparky, with the highest number being on the underside of those floppy ears, we counted them and threw them into the gasoline at the bottom of the can. Every time we counted 10 we put a scratch into the dirt. This rather pain-staking process took about 30 minutes and we covered every inch of that dog's hide. Amazingly enough the dog was very cooperative; it was as if he wanted us to remove those wood ticks. How many wood ticks did we remove? 276. Yes, 276. I couldn't believe it. After letting Sparky get up and run off, Ric took out a book of matches and lit the gasoline. That entire process had quite an impact on me, being only 12, and all the way home I kept repeating that number, 276, and wondered about wild animals having to endure those wood ticks every summer and losing all that blood.

While writing this chapter, and remembering that number of 276 wood ticks, I began to wonder if maybe I recalled incorrectly, because that number seemed so high. So, I called Cousin Ric and reminded him of that day. He could not remember what the number was but did recall it being a large number. Ric also reminded me that he had over 25 ticks on his own body once after a couple of hours in the woods. Coincidently, while finishing this chapter and including Ric's input, the Detroit Free Press included an article in the sports pages about Isle Royale's (an island in Lake Superior) decreasing populations of moose and wolves. Most interestingly, one of the factors apparently contributing to the decreasing moose population was ticks. According to the article, a single moose can have "tens of thousands" of ticks on it, severely weakening the animal to the point of being unable to fight off a wolf pack. So, if a moose can have thousands of ticks, a dog can seemingly have over 200. Thus that number of 276 may very well be correct and my memory was accurate.

Wood ticks were a common phenomenon when I was a youth. After a period of time in the woods, it would be necessary to examine one's body for ticks, if not immediately then later, when taking a sauna, or when getting ready for bed. It was not unusual for a wood tick to fall off one's body onto the table or even onto a food plate. The tick would be picked up and disposed of. We didn't worry about tick-transmitted diseases. Once while in the sauna my grandfather noticed a wood tick on my back and tried to pull it off. "Hey," I said, "that is not a wood tick." Without his reading glasses he mistook a birthmark (mole) for a wood tick and he was very insistent on pulling it off. One day one of my buddies was complaining about some pain in his hand. We took a look and when he spread his fingers, there was a wood tick, half swollen with blood, between his big finger and ring finger. We carefully removed it without bursting it and disposed of it in the wood stove. My mother asked me later if my buddy ever washed his hands and I had to admit that it probably was not very often. When would a young farm boy have time to wash his hands?

On the first weekend of grouse hunting season, Cousin Ric asked me to join him "partridge" (grouse) hunting. Most often it was just referred to as "bird" hunting. Ric had a 20 GA shotgun and I had my 410 GA. We began by walking, quite briskly, around a very large clear cut area, many acres in size, that was just beginning to show some growth of aspen and various kinds of shrubs. Outside of the clearing was good grouse habitat. A feeder stream of Black Crick flowed along the outside of this clearing and there was a fishing hole there that in fact was named, "The

Clearing." Uncle Willy took me there early in the summer and showed me how to fish that hole; we caught many brook trout at The Clearing through the years. Sparky flushed up 3 grouse within the first 2 hours and Ric took one shot but missed the bird. I did not get off a shot. Then, coming around the far side of the clearing, we heard Sparky barking quite aways off. Ric and I walked over to Sparky as fast as we could and, sure enough, there was a grouse perched in an aspen tree with Sparky underneath barking excitedly. Ric surveyed the area and said, "if we flush that grouse from the tree I think we can get a good shot at it. Get ready." We walked side by side toward the grouse with shotguns ready and, when it flushed, we both fired. The grouse crumpled, dropped to the ground, and was quickly found by Sparky who retrieved it. "Good dog, Sparky," Ric said to the dog, and scratched him behind the ears. Then to me he said, "Hey Jim! We finally bagged a grouse and you can take it home for dinner." I thought it was unlikely my 410 had anything to do with bagging that grouse but Ric never raised the question. Like Uncle Willy, he made abundant use of the word "we" when hunting and fishing with me along.

I cleaned that grouse, Uncle Willy having taught me how the previous autumn, and my mother cooked it. We had delicious baked grouse for our evening meal. Most of the eatable meat on a grouse was in the breasts, those powerful flight and drumming muscles. The legs contained dark meat but there wasn't much to them. The wings had so little meat they were discarded.

It was clear that Sparky had become a very good grouse dog and many grouse were bagged with the help of that dog. Ric told me during our recent phone conversation that one fall he bagged a large number of grouse and Sparky caught a few all by himself. Sparky apparently had a very "soft" mouth and would bring the grouse to Ric still alive. Most of my hunting was done alone, without a dog, but I remember bagging more than one grouse on the wing with just that 410 GA shotgun and 3 inch, # 6 shells. I still have that old shotgun and occasionally use it for grouse hunting. Carrying that old 410 bolt action with a 3 shell clip sure brings back many great memories, one being Sparky and the 276 wood ticks.

Chapter Five
Grouse, Chimneys and a Cap Shoot

Art, Matt, Jerry and I were the best of buddies and we did a variety of things together throughout the year, including basketball, swimming, touch football, card playing, and fishing and hunting. On this pleasant Saturday afternoon in October, the four of us got together with our shotguns for some grouse hunting. It was a brisk day so we all wore caps and jackets. Art had a 12 GA single shot, Jack a 20 GA 4 shot pump-action, and Matt and I had 410 GA four shot bolt action shotguns. Matt and I were just a little envious of Art having a 12 GA already at 16 yrs of age. Uncle Willy had recommended a 410 for me when I began hunting at age 14 and while it was quite adequate, there was something about a 12 GA that made it a most desirable shotgun for grouse and rabbits and with slugs or buckshot it served well for deer hunting too.

Any experienced grouse hunter would have said that four 16 year olds hunting together are going to have a slim chance of bagging a grouse, especially since we didn't have a grouse dog. We were aware of that view but we enjoyed the camaraderie when the 4 of us were together and, besides, we actually had bagged grouse before as a hunting foursome, even Matt and I with our 410s. It may have been during those years when grouse were at or near the peak of their 10 year population cycle. Art was clearly the "leader" of the 4 of us, with Jerry, Matt and me about equivalent as "followers."

Near all of our homes and even within our farm acreage there were forests with grouse, deer, and rabbits so it was not difficult to find hunting areas. Only Matt did not live on a farm but his home was nevertheless surrounded by farms and forests. The previous hunting season Matt had even bagged a grouse from a tree in his backyard, something to this day he is not proud of. Furthermore, Matt's dad was a logger so Matt knew the whereabouts of literally thousands of acres of hunting land.

Art, Jerry, and Matt arrived at 9 AM and my mother insisted all of us have a sugared donut fresh from the oven before we went out hunting. Not much arm-twisting was necessary. After the delicious donut with coffee for Jerry and me and milk for Art and Matt, we headed into the woods kitty corner from our farm. The owner of this forested area was not known to me and I never saw anyone there. The land was not posted and provided me with a nearby hunting area of 80 acres. It was excellent grouse habitat containing aspen and white birch for food (grouse eat the buds), several old logging roads to provide clover (more food) and gravel to aid the bird's gizzard for grinding up the buds and clover, and evergreens for cover. Uncle Willy had explained the food and cover requirements of grouse to me years earlier, as I tagged after him while out "bird" hunting.

We had all learned hunting safety procedures, me from Uncle Willy and the other three from their fathers and/ or uncles. We might have been better off splitting up into pairs but we seldom did that and preferred to hunt as a foursome. We took turns leading as we walked the logging roads, one after the other, with at least 10 feet between us. When I led we always moved along faster, even though the guys tried to slow me down. The rule we all understood was that the one leading got the shot; the other three of us didn't even raise our shotguns unless the grouse happened to flush from the side or flush from in front but then fly back in our direction. Such a flushed grouse might have 4 shotguns firing at it simultaneously. The sun was out so we knew our directions; furthermore I was quite familiar with these woods so even if it had been cloudy, there was no danger of getting lost. Amazingly enough, we flushed 3 grouse, twice when Jerry was leading and once when Art was leading. In none of those cases was there a clean shot. But Art, when he was leading, fired away with his 12 GA at a grouse that was out of range and already rapidly heading into a thicket. We all realized that he no doubt missed the bird completely but nevertheless we walked through the woods where the grouse had flushed and searched for feathers or a dead bird. We found nothing but it was always possible the dead grouse had fallen among some ferns and leaves and was so camouflaged we couldn't spot it. That happened more frequently when hunting without a dog. Art insisted he had a clean shot but the other three of us knew better.

After a couple of hrs, still hunting as a foursome and now in the far reaches of this 80 acres, farther in then I had ventured previously, we came upon an old hunting cabin. This cabin had probably been used a few decades earlier but now was quite decrepit; we all noted that the chimney was tilted and almost rusted through. We stopped and quietly surveyed the cabin and we each in our minds pictured hunters here years ago, maybe with a buck or two hanging from a tree branch, smoke coming out of the chimney. We then peeked in the windows and noted an old double bunk, mostly rotted away, a table, and an old box stove that had fallen over as the floor had decomposed. There were remnants of a woodpile. Brush was growing around the cabin and the windows had long since been broken through or shot through by other hunters. Only a few pieces of glass remained in the corners of the windows and the roof had collapsed on one side.

It was abundantly clear that no one was ever going to use this ramshackle cabin again. Art called us to the side, about 25 yards from the cabin and asked us to line up. "Why?" we asked. "Because we are going to shoot the chimney down," he said, and then added, " Jim and Matt, you guys fire first and see what you can do with those 410s." With some trepidation, Matt and I aimed, Art counted "1,2,3, fire," and we fired our 410s at the chimney, essentially simultaneously. Dust rose as the chimney tilted some more and partially collapsed on itself. "OK, Jerry, it looks like you and I are going to have to bring it down the rest of the way." "I think we might be able to do that," said Jerry. Art asked Matt and me to count down. As we counted Art and Jerry aimed, both shotguns fired and the chimney blew apart. We all laughed and reloaded. I don't know if the other fellows felt any remorse over that shooting but I felt guilt to a small degree. There was something about shooting someone else's chimney, even if it was old and decrepit, that bothered me just a little. But the guilt feeling did not last long.

We were still in the mood to do some more shooting and Jerry suggested some target practice, maybe shooting at some old stumps. Matt came up with the bright idea of shooting at something we throw up in the air, making it a little more challenging. "OK," I asked, "but what are we going to throw?" Then Art suggested we take turns throwing our caps up and shoot at them. He said, "A few BB holes won't be noticed and won't affect the caps any." After some hesitation we agreed it might be fun and established the rules; the thrower would be behind the shooter and would throw his cap over the head of the shooter on the count of three. We pulled long sticks to determine who would shoot first and who would throw first. We laid our shotguns down and threw our caps a few times just to see if we could give each cap some elevation and distance. All seemed about equivalent.

I was first to throw and Jerry was first to shoot; I got off a good throw and he fired. He may have hit my cap with a few BBs but there was no damage to the cap. "Wait until next time," Jerry said. Then Jerry threw and I fired at his cap with my 410. It seemed to be a clean miss. My thought was that this was going to be more difficult than it seemed, probably a good thing in that all our caps would be "saved" from damage. Such was not going to be the case. Next it was Art's turn to throw and Matt's turn to shoot. Art had a good arm and maybe a little heavier cap, or at least more aerodynamic, and before Matt could get a shot off, Art's cap sailed right toward a maple tree and hung up on a branch about 10 feet off the ground, swinging slightly like a sitting duck. Without hesitation Matt took good aim and blasted it with his 410. Art's cap flew backwards off the branch about 5 feet and came to rest on the ground.

Jerry and I chuckled and Jerry said, "Alright Matt, good shot." Art was obviously upset that Matt had shot at his cap while it was hung up in the tree but he didn't immediately say anything; certainly he did not join us in chuckling or in congratulating Matt. He just stood there fuming. Then Art looked at Matt and said, "Hey! You blasted my cap while it was just hanging there!" Before Matt could react, Art grabbed Matt's cap, marched over to a tree and hung the cap on a broken branch. With a stern look on his face, Art stepped back about 15 feet, aimed his 12 GA at Matt's cap, which was hanging there innocently, and blew it to smithereens!

GROUSE, DEER, AND UNCLE WILLY

The fun of shooting each other's caps turned serious. *Matt shot Art's cap with his 410 GA shotgun after it accidentally got caught in a tree. Then Art snatched Matt's cap, deliberately hung it in a tree, and blasted it to smithereens with his 12 GA shotgun. Matt could only watch in consternation. An old abandoned cabin, now without a chimney, is in the background.*

There was a moment of silence as we realized what had happened. Then Matt walked over and retrieved what was left of his cap. He held it up toward Jerry and me, as if to insure that we witnessed this dastardly deed by Art. Then Jerry spoke up rather loudly and said, "Alright Art! Good shot." This struck us as funny and all of us, even Matt, got to laughing and laughing. We must have laughed for a good 5 minutes. Then Matt placed what remained of his cap on his head and we laughed some more. Finally, Jerry said he had to get going as it was getting near milking time so we headed back to my house. I suggested that we keep quiet about shooting our caps and the chimney as our parents might not approve. I was thinking about what Uncle Willy would say to me if he found out, after drumming hunting safety and responsibility into me. I didn't dare tell him about this day.

For years afterwards, one of the four of us would bring up this incident from time to time and we would laugh and laugh, still clearly picturing Art blasting Matt's cap to smithereens with his 12 GA. On more than one of these occasions, Matt would say to Art, "You are lucky I only had a 410." Art would chuckle but never rub it in to Matt, I think because he realized a small degree of unfairness, having the 12 GA, but there was no evidence of much if any guilt.

Chapter Six
The Hunting Camp

Our family hunting "camp" consisted of a small cleared-out area, a primitive cabin, a spring for water, a latrine (in the opposite direction from the spring), and sufficient wood piled up to last through the hunting season. The site for the hunting camp was recommended by my late father who had hunted in this area for several years. The site chosen was within the vast acreage of a mining company. The location of the camp was based on the abundance of deer in the general area but bears, grouse and rabbits were also present. It had to be reasonably accessible initially by foot and later by tractor but still some distance from "civilization." A source of spring water nearby was also an important factor. The forest around the camp included virgin timber (hemlock, birch and maple), cedar, spruce, and balsam mainly in swamps, and new growth called slashing, which was mostly aspen. There were hills, valleys, and low land. It was prime hunting country. No permission was obtained to establish the site, which was in a remote area of the forest. I'm quite sure the thinking was that the mining company could not police such a vast area anyway.

The first effort to build a cabin required walking the roughly 3 miles to the site along an old logging road while carrying tools and supplies, including a roll of tar paper for the roof. It was tough going. The initial crew heading there to clear a spot and erect a cabin consisted of my father, who had identified the potential site and knew how to get there, Uncle Willy, who was 16, his brother Ralph who was several years older, and their father (my grandfather). They utilized cedar and hemlock logs for the walls and filled the open spaces between the logs with moss to keep the wind out. They brought no boards along so they split logs to make the roof, which they then covered with tar paper. By the end of the day with the walls up and the roof on, the four fellows could see the potential for a decent hunting cabin. It wasn't adequate enough to spend the night so they hiked back out late in the afternoon.

An old water barrel that was modified to be a stove, some stove piping, glass for a window and boards and hinges for a door, were carried in on subsequent trips.

In May, after the end of WWII, Uncle Willy, his brother Ralph, their father, and Cousin Ric, established a crude road to the camp. Cousin Ric drove his dad's (Ralph's) ford tractor with a single axle trailer behind. It took some road clearing by everyone and required much effort just to get there. When they weren't clearing the road the other three rode in the trailer or walked behind. The trailer was loaded with lumber, plaster, a roll of tar paper, and tools. The cabin roof was solidified and re-papered, plaster replaced the old dried moss between the wall logs, and shelves were constructed along one wall and one somewhat wider shelf served double duty as a table. Sitting stools without backs were constructed. A single wide bed was constructed across the end of the cabin; hunters slept side by side.

Plenty of deer and other game animals were to be harvested at this camp and many adventures were to take place. Additional trips with the tractor and trailer were forthcoming through the years to deliver materials, including boards for a crude wooden floor. The game warden once arrested and fined one of my uncles for riding in the trailer with a loaded rifle. Via a rather round-about route from the east, it was possible to drive a car within a half mile of the camp. Still, it was much faster than walking in along the original route that was utilized for the tractor.

During one hunting season Uncle Willy recalled that 3 large bucks were shot on opening day down the hill from the camp. Those bucks had to be dragged up that hill to the camp. It was customary to utilize the heart and kidneys of the first buck for a stew, also containing potatoes, carrots, and rutabaga, that provided nourishment for the hunters for several days. After getting them to camp, those 3 bucks then had to be dragged the three miles to civilization and a car, brought to the farm and processed. Most of the meat was canned if the weather was not cold enough to freeze it. Uncle Willy said, "It was a big effort but the deer meat was important. After all, there were many mouths to feed on the farm." Uncle Willy was one of 14 children.

I got to the camp for the first time when I was 13. Uncle Willy took me and two of my buddies, Ron and Don, for a 2 night stay there in September. No hunting seasons were open except for varmints. Uncle Willy drove his car as close as possible using the round-about route from the east and we walked in the last half mile along an old logging road. We flushed three grouse almost immediately and about halfway to the camp Uncle Willy stopped us and whispered, "Look! There are two deer behind that windfall!" They looked at us and we looked at them for several minutes. Then Uncle Willy gave a "blow" like a deer and they spooked. With their white tails held high, they ran over a ridge and into a cedar swamp. We didn't see any antlers. Uncle Willy carried his bolt action 22 rifle and allowed us boys to take our Daisy BB guns and sling shots. None of us knew quite what to expect. As we arrived at the camp, Uncle Willy spotted a porcupine high up in a tree near the cabin. Because porcupines had gotten into the cabin and chewed on the table, he immediately brought the porky down with one shot from his 22. It dropped heavily to the ground and we got a close-up look at it. Uncle Willy showed us some quills and explained how the porcupine can protect its vulnerable belly from predators by rolling up on itself.

It was rather dark inside the cabin as there was only one small window. Using a wooden match, Uncle Willy lit the single kerosene lamp. There was a bed made of boards across the back end, with a thin mattress-like material along its width; we unloaded our gear onto it. Uncle Willy put the food we brought on a shelf and instructed Ron and Don to fetch some firewood. "Make sure you bring some birch bark," he said. At the same time he said to me, "Jim, I need you to fetch some water." He gave me a pail and told me where the spring was. What a beautiful, clean, cold-water spring. This spring was the headwaters of a small brook trout crick called Finney Crick that was a tributary to Black Crick. It was a crick Uncle Willy and I fished often, particularly at "The Clearing" hole, but far downstream from the headwater spring at the camp site. I didn't know about the origin of Finney Crick until the day I called to wish Uncle Willy a happy 91st birthday. Naturally we talked about hunting and fishing and one subject that came up was the hunting camp and the spring.

The hunting cabin. Uncle Willy, standing in the low doorway of the hunting cabin, sent Jim to fetch water from the spring and Ron and Don to fetch firewood from the wood pile. Unloaded rifles and BB guns were kept outside the cabin under the overhang of the roof out of the rain or snow.

It was getting to be late afternoon so Uncle Willy built a fire in the pot-bellied stove, showing us how to do it by first lighting the birch bark. He then opened 2 cans of chicken noodle soup with a hand-held can opener, poured the soup into an old pot that was blackened from soot on the outside and added water. To heat the soup, the pot was placed on a flattened spot on the top of the stove. The stove also had a lid which could be removed so that a pot or pan could be exposed directly to the fire. The stove gave off a good amount of heat and the fall chill in the air quickly dissipated. Unexpectedly, some pieces of wood from the ceiling, previously blackened from earlier fires, fell into the soup pot, causing Uncle Willy to mutter to himself (I thought maybe some swear words), and he scooped them out as best he could with a spoon. We ate that "burned" tasting soup and homemade bread with butter for dinner, with coffee and water to drink, and apples for dessert. No complaints from us boys. I quickly realized that life at the hunting camp was going to be quite primitive compared to at the farm, the latter not being exactly plush.

In the morning, after a fitful night for all of us sleeping on a rather hard surface, Uncle Willy made coffee by adding coffee grounds to boiling water, then letting the mix settle. The coffee strainer did not get all of the grounds out but it was good tasting coffee. Breakfast was bread and jelly with dry cereal. I don't ever recall having milk at the hunting camp. That day we did quite a lot of hiking and all the while scouting for signs of deer. We chased up deer, grouse and rabbits but did not shoot any. Uncle Willy showed us areas where deer had browsed and said, "When deer chew off branches they leave the ends jagged whereas rabbits cut off the branch ends cleanly. Deer of course can browse higher, sometimes getting up on their hind legs to reach tender cedar branches." Uncle Willy showed us the deer "browse line," i.e. the maximum height deer can reach to browse. Back then, deer fed mainly, if not exclusively, on browse and thus venison had a distinct "wild" taste, compared to venison of the corn-, soybean-, and alfalfa-fed deer today. When we returned to the camp we did some target practicing with Uncle Willy's 22. Naturally he was the most accurate shooter but he gave us boys suggestions to get better, like to not flinch when we pulled the trigger.

At the end of our short stay, we cleaned up the cabin as best we could, which included washing the dishes and putting them away. We had eaten every bit of food we brought. It would have been nice to supplement our food with a rabbit, which Uncle Willy had in mind, but he wasn't able to shoot one. At one point we considered a porcupine, which Uncle Willy said was very tasty, but we boys talked him out of that idea. It was a great two day adventure and none of us, including Uncle Willy, was anxious to head back home.

I was able to obtain a deer hunting license at the age of 14. That fall, Uncle Willy took Cousin Ric, who was 17, my buddy Dirk, and me to the hunting camp for a few days at the beginning of deer hunting season, Nov. 15-18. There was about a half foot of snow and we could see plenty of tracks as we walked in the half mile from Uncle Willy's car, each of us carrying a back pack loaded with food and gear. Hunter orange was not utilized back then and instead hunters wore dark red plaid coats and hats. Its a wonder more hunters did not get shot because the red plaid looked black in low light. We chased up three deer as we walked in and while none had antlers, my heart raced as they disappeared amongst the trees. Only bucks were legal game. Both Dirk and I were impressed that Uncle Willy and Ric had their rifles aimed at those deer within a split second. Uncle Willy reminded us that a hunter had to be ready at all times because one never knew when game would appear. Dirk and I each had a lever-action 22 rifle, hardly powerful enough to bring down a deer with a body shot but a shot into the head could be effective. Uncle Willy coached us about that – reminding us not to shoot without a clear head shot available. I don't think he thought either of us was ready to bag a deer but that some time at the hunting camp would be a good experience for us. Uncle Willy and Ric each carried 30-30 lever-action carbines. All of our rifles had open sights as telescopic sights were not popular yet.

The first day out hunting, probably about 25 degrees, Uncle Willy took Dirk and me with him. For various periods of time, usually not exceeding an hour, he placed us together or singly in "posting" positions. Ric hunted alone all day. We saw no deer all morning. We all came into camp for lunch and a short break to warm up our feet. Even with adequate winter boots and wool socks my feet still got cold so I added an extra pair of socks for the afternoon. We then headed back out hunting but again we did not see any deer. After hunting the early part of the afternoon, but in a different location, Uncle Willy brought Dirk and me back to camp at about 3:00 PM and headed out on his own. I can see why he wanted some "alone" hunting time. Uncle Willy could sit perfectly still for a long time. In contrast, Dirk and I undoubtedly moved around far too much and probably were noisy too, especially me. With their keen senses, deer could undoubtedly hear us and see us. Dirk and I played cards for the remainder of the afternoon with light from the single kerosene lamp and we kept the box stove fired up with wood. At one point we heard 3 faint shots, muffled by the cabin walls.

Uncle Willy arrived back at camp first, just at dark, and reported seeing no deer but hearing some shots. He said, "I hope Ric got his buck." A few minutes later Ric appeared and he was clearly excited. He had seen a nice buck, maybe a six pointer he thought, and had gotten 3 shots off at it as it raced between the trees. But after examining its tracks he did not see blood and so assumed all 3 shots missed. Uncle Willy said, "Don't feel bad, I have missed many bucks myself. Maybe one of us will bag that buck tomorrow. It won't leave the area."

Later in the evening after a meal of meat, potatoes, carrots and bread, I fetched water for the dishes and for morning coffee. We talked awhile and Uncle Willy told us a story about shooting an 8 point buck and having to follow its blood trail several hundred yards before being able to bag it with a killing shot. Then he told another story about a friend who had "buck fever." Buck fever, he said, "is a condition wherein the hunter sees a buck but gets so excited he pumps his cartridges out of his rifle without firing them at the deer." Unfired cartridges have been found at those sites of "buck fever" proving the behavior as true, even though the hunter swears he/she shot at the buck. "In less severe cases of buck fever," Uncle Willy explained, "the hunter fires his rifle but is so nervous he could not hit the broad side of a barn from 20 feet."

To Dirk and me, buck fever was an astonishing behavior and we quietly contemplated such a situation occurring. After a short spell, Dirk asked, quite innocently, "Ric, do you think maybe you had a case of buck fever when you saw that buck today?" The teasing had begun. Oh boy, did Ric ever get hot under the collar from that remark and emphatically said, "No, I didn't have buck fever!" After a few minutes, Dirk said in Ric's direction, "We think you must have had buck fever," and then we both giggled. Now

Ric really got angry. He first grabbed Dirk and with the knuckle of his big finger repeatedly punched him on the upper arm muscle, just below the shoulder and asked Dirk, "Did I have buck fever, huh, did I?" Dirk, in agony, quickly answered, "No, no, you didn't." Then Ric did the same to me and I quickly said, "No, no, you didn't have buck fever." Uncle Willy smiled through all of this knowing we were just teasing Ric. Then Dirk and I looked at each other, giggled, and simultaneously said, "We think you had buck fever." This time the shoulder beating lasted longer and was more more intense. Again he made us say he didn't have buck fever and that we were sorry to suggest that he did. No more words about buck fever came forth because Ric's glare was very menacing. We could see Uncle Willy smiling and maybe he secretly enjoyed us teasing Ric. Dirk and I lost some sleep due to our shoulder muscles aching throughout the night. The next morning we each had a nice black and blue bruise where the beating took place..

Dirk and I agreed to not mention buck fever to Ric ever again but we have laughed about that experience many times through the years and we both still remember it vividly. What made the experience so funny was that of all hunters, Cousin Ric was the least likely to ever have buck fever. He was as mentally and physically tough as anyone. I have wanted to ask him if he was genuinely angry with Dirk and me or whether he realized that this was an opportunity to just have some fun and so he "acted" angry. Neither Dirk nor I have ever dared ask him that.

At the hunting camp we sometimes played a card game called "dog." Also, after a day of hunting near the farm and after the farm chores were completed, some of us boys would get together at one of our houses for a few games of dog during the evening. The origin of this game is unknown although I admit to not searching it out thoroughly. The game is played with anywhere from 2 to 7 people, with 8 and above making it somewhat unwieldy. The objective of the game is to get "out" and therefore not be left as the "dog," the last person left with cards. In other words, there is only one loser, the dog. The dog must withstand a certain amount of ridicule, might have to perform very undesirable but agreed upon tasks, or just quietly accept being left dog in that particular game, never a welcome thing. At the hunting camp the last person to be left "dog" accepted all the other dogs of the evening and also had to go to the spring and fetch water for morning coffee. That meant putting on one's boots, coat and hat and heading out into the cold and dark with a flashlight and water bucket. It was a competitive game but all in fun! If after a stay of a few days at the hunting camp a person did not get left dog at least once, it was indeed a very successful camp stay.

James Woodsing

Who is the dog? *Jim is playing a card game, called Dog, with 3 of his buddies. Jim got left with cards and therefore became the "dog." Jim, in the spirit of fun and to act out a dog's behavior, climbed up onto the table, uttering "woof, woof" and lifted his leg to (pretend) pee on Ron, causing Ron to back out of the line of fire. The other boys tease Jim and yell out "bow wow" and point at him.*

Chapter Seven
Compass Use:
Who Made Those Tracks?

Much of the time when I was out hunting with Uncle Willy, with others, or alone, there were roads or other landmarks nearby that indicated quite clearly where we were, even on a cloudy day. We are talking about the 1940's and 1950's, way before GPS or cell phones had been invented. We had a compass, common sense, and the power of observation. Uncle Willy instructed me to understand how a compass worked and reminded me more than once to always carry one in the woods, even when going fishing. "Never use it next to objects that are made of steel, like your rifle," Uncle Willy said, "They are magnetic and will influence the compass needle." Then he told me about a time when he wandered away from a crick on a cloudy day to pick raspberries and before he knew it, he had lost his bearings and his fishing rod, packsack, and bait can, which he had laid down beside the crick. Fortunately he had a compass and found his way back to the crick; he had ended up more than a quarter mile from the crick without realizing it. Another important point Uncle Willy made was how to walk in a straight line in the woods, the strategy being to find a tree or other structure in the direction one wanted to walk, and then sight a 2nd tree in the same line from the first tree. When reaching the first tree, a 3rd tree would be identified in the same line, and so forth, occasionally checking one's compass to be sure to not wander off course.

Uncle Ned also instructed me on using a compass once, when I was probably only 9 or 10 and hardly understood the various directions: north, south, east and west. I knew about the North Star and the Northern Lights, but really did not understand anything about the magnetic north pole, the earth's movements, position of the sun, why we had seasons, and other natural phenomena. Anyway, one evening just prior to the opening of deer season, Uncle Ned and Aunt Kitty came over to visit. Back then, in this farming community, since we did not have phones, it was customary to just decide to visit someone and away you would go. Thus one had to always be ready for evening company, with homemade biscuits and donuts at the ready. After coffee and donuts, and a game of checkers, Uncle Ned took out a new compass. "I brought you your very own compass," he said. "Wow, thank you," I said, and I looked at my mother and she smiled. I still have that compass and it still works just fine. And magnetism is still a puzzle for physicists. It was the kind of compass that had a tightening screw that would lock the needle in place so that it would not flop around in your pocket. To use it one had to unlock the needle, hold it level, and the needle would find north. Then the compass would be turned so that the N on the dial was at the arrow end of the needle. Thus all the directions would be indicated. "Here, I'll show you how to use this compass," Uncle Ned said, and he got everyone's attention, right at the kitchen table. "First you hold it level," he said and held it in his fingers so the needle would freely rotate to find north; it settled in place. Then he asked my mother if that was in fact north on our farm, and she said yes. "Now," he said, "if you hold the compass still while the needle is pointing north, and tighten the screw down, from then on this compass will always point north." Everyone was silent for a moment while I digested this thought. Then I said, "No way, what if you happened to be facing south when you took the compass out of your pocket?" And, I was serious. Everyone laughed and I realized it was Uncle Ned's idea of humor.

Before we would head off into the woods, Uncle Willy would take out his compass and check the directions. He would observe what direction a road was heading and what direction we were going when entering the hunting area. Then he would ask me, "if you realize you don't know for sure how to get to our car and to this road, in what direction will you walk?" I would look at the compass, and come up with an answer. He would agree or ask, "Think about where we are again. Are you sure that is the direction you would walk?" Only if I couldn't figure it out would he finally correct me.

As I mentioned in an earlier chapter, my father died in an automobile accident when I was six months old. When I was 15 my mother remarried. Fortunately, my stepfather was a hunter and a good woodsman. I had already acquired a 30-30 Winchester carbine lever action rifle with open sights. One Saturday near the end of deer hunting season, I joined Uncle Willy, my stepfather, and Hans, a family friend, to hunt. Only bucks were legal to shoot in those days. After the morning farm chores, we headed out into six inches of fresh snow. The forest was just beautiful with snow on every branch and everything quiet and clean; there was no wind. It was a cloudy day and a few flurries were still in the air. It was about 25 degrees, a very comfortable hunting temperature. I was to be the deer "driver" which made sense because I struggled to sit or stand still while posting. Our strategy was to have me get dropped off at an old logging road and I would walk in about a quarter of a mile and wait 30 minutes. The other 3 would continue north about a half mile, park the car, and they would take positions as "posters" along another old logging road that was going east into forest owned by a mining company. I waited the 30 minutes to give them time to be positioned, then I walked in going east about a quarter mile and at that point started walking north toward the 3 fellows who were the "posters."

The wind was non-existent so it was mainly my noise and presence that was going to be driving the deer as I headed toward the posters. It was not necessary to hoot and holler but only to walk slowly and occasionally break a branch or two, sufficient noise to spook deer. It was real thick forest and heavy going so I just took my time. There were some fresh deer tracks, recognizable because they were not filled with fresh snow. Thus deer had been moving after the snow fall, perhaps very recently. I trudged along heading north, or at least I thought I was heading north. After about 15 minutes of walking around evergreens and windfalls covered with snow, and through nice timber but also through slashings of aspen, I came upon fresh human tracks. I stopped and looked at these tracks. They were so fresh I thought the person making these tracks must be very close so I looked around and listened. There was no movement and no sound. I then realized that the tracks looked a little bit familiar and, sure enough, they matched my own boot tracks exactly. These were my own tracks! I had indeed made a large circle and had come upon my own tracks. I was really dumbfounded. Sure enough, after checking my compass, I was heading almost directly back toward where I had begun the deer drive. The snow was so thick on the trees and windfalls that I had completely lost track of my directions. It did not occur to me to question the accuracy of my compass because Uncle Willy had warned me about that several times. He would say, "you must trust your compass," and he would tell me a different story every time about hunters who would get lost because they thought their compass was not working properly. I scolded myself, took a careful compass reading, and continued the drive, occasionally checking my compass to make sure I was heading north.

James Woodsing

Whose tracks are these? Jim ponders over a fresh set of hunter's tracks in the snow. He wonders how another hunter could be so close to him this early in the morning and looks around for the fellow. Jim scratches his head, looks at his compass, studies the tracks again, and realizes he has walked in a circle and has come upon his own tracks.

After another 10 minutes, I came upon tracks of 3 deer that I had clearly spooked up as the tracks indicated the deer were running. Then I heard a rifle shot not too far away. I stopped for a few minutes but there were no more shots. After another 10 minutes or so I came upon the old logging road the "posters" were on. I looked left and right and there was Uncle Willy. He gave me a short wave and I proceeded to where he was standing. Sort of in a whisper, he said, "You chased out 3 deer and one of them was a small buck. It stopped just before the road, right over there near that windfall, and I downed it with one shot. I haven't dressed it yet. I was waiting so you could see how its done." We walked to the small buck, a 5 pointer, and Uncle Willy skillfully and efficiently dressed it, taking only about 15 minutes. I watched the process closely. We left the buck there and as we walked further east we came upon my step-father posting under a tree. He and Hans had each seen a doe, which I had probably also chased out. We continued hunting until noon but saw no more deer. Then we dragged the buck to where the car was parked. All in all it was a successful morning of hunting and I had learned the importance of having a compass and trusting it to tell me the directions. "Good job of driving deer," Uncle Willy said to me as we got into the car.

There were plenty of times I got twisted around in the woods, both while fishing and hunting. Fortunately I never had to spend the night in the woods, waiting for someone to come and rescue me. At the hunting camp one November I was temporarily lost and it was getting near twilight. I actually began thinking about spending the night in the woods, a scary thought. I had to stop, talk to myself and say, "Don't panic Jim, think," and, sure enough, I found my way out. When it is below the freezing mark, there is snow on the ground, and there is wind, it is not pleasant to think about a night in the woods alone. What a great feeling to see that familiar land mark, your car, a road, crick or fence, and realize exactly where you are.

While talking with Uncle Willy on the phone in Jan., 2009, I asked him if he had ever been lost and maybe had to spend the night in the woods. He said, "No, I've never been really lost. I've been twisted around but I always found my way out. I always had a compass and forced myself to believe it." He recalled one day fishing on the Big Lake (Lake Superior) with a friend, on the friend's boat, and a fog enveloped them. They decided it would be good to get close enough to shore to see land and then make their way to the harbor. The friend, the boat's owner, thought the boat's compass was not working correctly and wanted to go north, which would have taken them farther out into the lake. Uncle Willy sternly told him to believe his compass, which the friend reluctantly did, and they made it close enough to shore to see land and the river harbor, thus finding their way out of the fog.

Chapter Eight
Practicing Survival

Plenty has been written about survival in the wilderness and some people, including my oldest son, take pride in doing just that, testing survival skills even in the middle of winter with much snow on the ground. Of course it helps to be prepared in advance, anticipating spending a night or more in the out of doors. But what if you are a hunter, a hiker, or a fisherman, and realize you are lost and thus face a night in the forest alone, not having given much thought to being lost? It would help if one has at least done some mental preparation and some reading, and better if one has actually practiced. In Outdoor Life (Feb., 2009), Rich Johnson summarized the main points regarding wilderness survival taken from his book, "Guide to Wilderness Survival" (McGraw Hill). These are: 1. Take a deep breath and gather your thoughts. 2. Assess your situation; think about what you have to do. 3. Take action. 4. Make a camp, the main thing being to find or build a shelter. 5. Build a fire. 6. Get some rest; sleep if you can. 7. Eat something as both your brain and muscles need energy. In Field and Stream (Jan., 2009), Keith McCafferty suggests the person lost should think and act in terms of a 3 day plan. On day 1, recognize you are lost and stay calm. Fight the urge to panic and maintain a sense of inner peace. Assume there will be search and rescue efforts to find you. Stop walking so that you do not leave the search area. Establish a home base. Finally, build a fire for the night. On day 2, begin signaling the searchers (3 fires making smoke; 3 shots; 3 whistles). On the afternoon of day 2, if still not found, build a shelter, gather more wood, try to find or provide clean water, and continue signaling. On day 3, gather more wood, re-enforce your shelter, collect more water, continue signaling, and stay put. You may take walks to look for familiar landmarks but always return to your home base. Ron Dawson in his book, Outsmart Outback II (2008, Integrity House Publishing, Ontario, OR), pretty much agrees with the above but in addition says the two most important activities when lost are to build a fire and build a shelter. He says a lost person should allow 1 hour to build a fire and 1-3 hours to build a shelter, depending on available materials. He then discusses details about building fires and shelters, the how and where.

Of the various suggestions above, my view is that finding or building a shelter is the most critical, especially if its cold, in the low 40's or below. And if its near 20 or colder, then a shelter is imperative. Furthermore, it may be too wet to start a fire, too dry to risk one, or there may not be firewood available. I decided to accept the challenge of finding or building a shelter on my own 40 acres. Mind you, I didn't do as my son suggested, "Spend the night, dad." No, I did this during the light of day and just wanted to test whether I could find or build a shelter that could keep me reasonably warm for several hours, to give me an idea of whether I might make it through a night. When my friend said, "You be careful; you could die out there," I realized most of us are not at all prepared for outdoors survival. I therefore set out on my 40 acres at noon on a 28 degree day on snowshoes with about a foot of snow on the ground, with a backpack in which I had 2 sheets of thin plastic (8x10 ft.), a light weight blanket, some newspapers, a sandwich, an energy bar, some nuts, a bottle of water, a hatchet, a small saw, and waterproof matches. I brought my 20 GA shotgun just for the comfortable feeling of having it. I was dressed for the weather, in layers, with thermal underwear, a warm coat, warm mittens, and water proof boots. I made sure snow was not forecast that day and that there wasn't much wind. There was no need to make the challenge too difficult. I walked into the middle of the 40 acres and stopped, fictitiously admitting I was lost, and then listing in my head the 7 points (see above) from Johnson's book.

I began to look for a shelter and realized immediately that one was not staring me in the face. So I began to snowshoe, with a plan in mind. After about 10 minutes, I had identified 3 potential shelters, each of which would require work to improve. The first was under the overhanging branches of a red pine tree, among the hundreds of red pines we had planted a dozen years ago. Snow had pulled the branches down on one side making a "cavity" underneath. But the branches over the cavity would only protect from an east wind and the prevailing winds were from the north west. Furthermore, there was a scarcity of firewood nearby. I moved on and came to possibility #2, which was a cavity inside a brush pile that was over a windfall, the roots of which closed off one end completely. The opening was facing east, away from the prevailing winds. The brush pile was left over from the clear-cut logging I had done that year. With some work I envisioned cleaning out the cavity so I could fit inside comfortably and even stretch out. There was firewood nearby. Some evergreen branches could be used to cover the opening after I got inside. I liked this possibility but decided to look further and came upon possibility #3, a felled pine about a foot in diameter that the loggers had not claimed. Snow had piled up around the branch-free trunk but there was space underneath that I could visualize myself crawling into. There was ample firewood nearby. But, this was a low spot and while it might be protected from the wind, the ground might be wet. I therefore back-tracked to #2 and studied it carefully. Ten minutes had elapsed looking for a possible shelter.

After taking off my snowshoes I began preparing site #2 for a fictitious night. I found a nearby hemlock and cut off as many branches as I could reach, trying not to get snow down my neck. With the hatchet and saw, I cut away some of the protruding sticks within the cavity and evened it out, sort of in the shape of a person. With my head inside, I could see that there were two holes letting snow in so I covered these with hemlock and cedar branches and piled snow on top of the branches using a snow shoe as a shovel. I gathered all the available dead and dried ferns and dead leaves from around the area and placed them on the floor of the cavity for insulation and comfort. The last of the hemlock and cedar branches I placed up and down in front of the cavity, effectively closing it off to the outside, except for a crawl-in space. I then backed myself in feet first and put my backpack under my head. Not bad I thought. Lying on my left side, facing the opening, I stayed in the shelter for a half hour and did not get chilled, even with the temperature at 28 degrees. However, I felt some cold on my knees and realized that my knees were wet from kneeling on the snow. Getting wet is frowned upon in all of the above source material and I was clearly reminded of that. When I crawled out I felt some soreness in my left hip, the one against the ground, but that was likely due to old age, not having padding and had nothing to do with losing heat to the ground.

It was time to plan for a fire. With snow on the ground I did not worry about the fire spreading. I set about gathering firewood but the only wood available was old and very dry. It would burn very quickly but likely give a lot of heat. The question was, which I asked myself out loud, "How much wood is needed to last a night?" I piled most of the "stock" wood next to the enclosed end of the shelter within reach from inside and prepared to build the fire just at the open end, where my head would be, even though McCafferty (see above) recommends a fire the length of one's body. I reasoned that a 6 foot long fire would require a lot of wood. I dragged three longer (12-15 feet) and thicker (3-4 inch diameter) dead trees to the camp site and leaned them against the end of the shelter. These I could cut into shorter lengths later or burn them from one end to the other. I put newspaper on the plastic and folded the blanket on top, then pushed them inside the cavity. I wanted a sandwich of plastic on the outside, a blanket inside of that, newspaper between the plastic and blanket underneath, and me in between with blanket and plastic above and blanket, newspaper, and plastic below, all on a bed of leaves and boughs. An idea I would like to try is to make a garbage bag sleeping bag, as described by Dolly Garza in Outdoor Survival Training Student Manual for Alaska's Youth (1993). One fills a large garbage bag with leaves, grass, reeds, and dried moss, a hole is dug in the middle and a second garbage bag is pushed into the hole. The person then crawls into the inside bag, keeping one's head outside to not accumulate breath moisture inside. Even if the garbage bag is short, one could at least get their feet and legs inside the make-shift sleeping bag..

Preparing the shelter and gathering wood for the fire together took 50 minutes. So adding the 10 minutes of time to search for a possible shelter, one hour had elapsed. It was important to keep track of the time because I wanted to know at what time one needed to decide that a night in the woods was going to occur. Dawson (see above) says a minimum of 2 hrs is necessary for these two activities. I saved an hour by finding an almost ready-made shelter but of course one cannot count on that kind of good fortune so more time should be allowed.

It was time to build a fire. With snow on the ground there was no danger of the fire spreading. Fortunately the windfall was a birch tree and therefore birth bark was readily available, a very good material for starting a fire. I cleared off the snow from a region about 3 feet from the shelter opening and started a fire there with the aid of the birch bark and dry sticks. Once the fire was underway I warmed myself sufficiently and concluded that a fire was indeed beneficial. Duh! Next I visualized it being close to dark, leaned my shotgun against a tree away from the fire but close enough whereby I could reach it from the opening, built up the fire with some larger pieces, and I crawled inside the shelter. With some effort, I got between the layers of blanket and plastic, facing the fire. I could feel the warmth of the fire on my face.

Practicing survival is an educational activity. *Jim identified this crawl space in a brush pile as a potential shelter. The shelter was improved by adding spruce branches and then snow to cover the two holes on the top and part of the side opening; he then gathered firewood and piled it in front, one pile for the fire and one for additional wood. Here Jim reaches out and makes sure he can add wood to the fire without leaving the protection of the shelter.*

After the fire burned down during the next hour I added some more wood from the stock pile and got it going again without having to exit the shelter. I then pulled some pine branches across the opening and laid there with my eyes closed in the semi-darkness, not yet feeling any cold. Amazingly enough I napped for maybe 20 minutes, reassuring myself that it might be possible to sleep for at least part of a night in this kind of shelter. After 3 hrs in the shelter, I began to feel some chill. After another half hour, not feeling any more or less chilled, I crawled out of the shelter and built up the fire again from remaining coals and warmed myself up. I used a suggestion from my nephew who lives in Anchorage which was to break off pieces of dried logs, if not too large diameter, by levering them between two trees that are close to each other. The logs could also be fed into the fire little by little from one end to the other, even several at a time. I also burned through longer pieces, which took 40 minutes, and then the piece burned off I added to the fire. With a 15 foot long log of 3 inches in diameter, one could burn through it at 5 foot intervals and thus acquire 3 pieces approximately 4 feet long. Burning through would utilize about one foot of the piece and provide heat at the same time. A 15 foot log of 3 inches average diameter would last for over 2 hrs. The more of these small diameter dead trees one could find the better. A total of 6 or 7 would keep a fire going pretty much through the night.

From the experience so far, I realized that in order to survive a night, it was imperative to have matches, a source of firewood, a hatchet, a blanket, and at least one sheet of plastic, ideally two. Newspaper would serve double as fire starting material and as insulation from the ground. While it would be a greater challenge if it was even colder and if there was a wind, and/or snow, sleet, or rain, and if it was near dark before accepting the overnight survival prospect, I concluded that it would be possible for me to survive a night. I'm going to try it.

Scott Shalaway writes for a local newspaper on nature topics. In the Jan. 15, 2009, issue, his title was "Hypothermia – a cold killer." He points out that the number one killer of outdoors enthusiasts is hypothermia and that most cases occur with temperatures between 30-50 degrees. The best treatment is prevention and most important is to stay dry and stay out of the wind. One must recognize when there is danger of hypothermia and then, as above, take the necessary action to survive.

Coincidently, a hunter was lost this past hunting season not far from our 40 acres. He had entered the woods at 6 AM with the temperature near 40 degrees and after 10 hours of hunting realized he was lost. He called his family and gave an approximate location. The family called 911 and county officers were dispatched. The GPS locater on the hunter's cell phone gave a location, not accessible by motor vehicles, but close enough so that a coast guard helicopter was able to rescue the hunter just before dark. He was treated for hypothermia at a local hospital and released the same evening. We wondered why he waited until near dark to call his family. It turns out there was a warrant for the man's arrest.

Speaking with Uncle Willy on the phone I told him about this fellow. Uncle Willy then recalled that when he was a youth, he remembered a big city fellow who came up north to hunt. A couple of days before deer hunting season opened, the fellow went out to "scout" for deer sign. When he did not return to meet his friends a search was begun and although the search continued into the following day the man was not located. Uncle Willy's father and many others participated in the search but to no avail. The day before hunting season began a man collecting ferns found the fellow's body, only a half mile from a black-topped county road. He had likely died of hypothermia.

Its one thing to survive being lost in the wilderness. What about being lost in everyday life? An article by Ben Sherwood appeared in Newsweek (Feb. 2, 2009),

"What It Takes To Survive." He writes about survival after illness, an accident, job loss, and other negative events in life. He concludes that only 10% of all people are really equipped mentally to survive these kinds of encounters. Perhaps wilderness survival might be easier for these same 10%. Regardless, with careful planning and thought, and especially practice, anyone can be prepared for a night in the woods.

Chapter Nine
The Rifle

In the 1920's, '30's, '40's and '50's, many local farmers and others living in our farming community resorted to providing meat for the table by shooting deer and other game even when hunting season was not open. Violating the game laws, which is called "violating" for short, was particularly prevalent during the years of the Great Depression. Even today, violations of game laws occur from time to time, but the fines and penalties have become very stiff and thus the deterrent is strong. Furthermore, poverty is not as widespread and meat is readily available in the grocery. But, back then, a 150 lb deer would provide enough meat for a poor family for quite some time. Refrigeration not being available, the meat was dried, salted, smoked, or canned to preserve it during warmer months.

Game law enforcers, presently called conservation officers, were called game wardens in those years and each warden had a large territory to police. Game wardens often knew the individuals who were the biggest violators and the violators knew the game wardens, often on a first name basis.

Uncle Willy often hunted and fished with my father, as they were brothers-in-law, and both knew the local woods like the backs of their hands, especially our 40 acres and the surrounding acreage. Uncle Willy was not known to be a violator but the same could not be said for my father who was well-known for his violating. At that time the cost of violating was jail time as most violators could not afford to pay fines, and the person's rifle was sometimes confiscated. Depending on the severity of the violation, the rifle was sometimes not returned to the violator. My father actually made it a "game" to match wits with the local game warden, a Mr. Smith, and for years managed to not get caught and apprehended for violating. Perhaps it was because he valued his rifle highly that he was so very careful.

My oldest sister relates from those years before I was born that our father's deer rifle, a 30-40 Krag, was as much a part of his life as his farm tools. Realizing the importance of having a well-functioning rifle, he apparently would often sit at the kitchen table, cleaning, oiling, and polishing it while my sisters watched every move in childish wonder. He never brought his cartridges inside, keeping them instead hidden out in the woodshed, out of their hands, a lesson in safety that my sisters took seriously.

One day in early fall, weeks before deer hunting season opened, my father was out violating, looking for a deer to provide meat for my sisters and our mother. Mr. Smith was there, knowing where my father liked to hunt, spied him and moved as quickly as possible through the forest to apprehend him. My father knew he was caught but he had seen Mr. Smith from afar and had time to hide his rifle under a windfall. As I pointed out above, my father knew every windfall, stump, dead tree, and live tree like the back of his hand. Yes, Mr. Smith made the arrest but in his haste did not search for my father's rifle. So, while Mr. Smith succeeded in having my father jailed, there was no rifle, and no evidence for a game law violation; therefore my father could not remain jailed for long.

Realizing that my father must have hidden the rifle, Mr. Smith planned to head back out to our 40 acres the next day. But, by that time, my mother had instructed my sisters to alert her father-in-law (our grandpa), about the rifle. Grandpa took his son Eddie (my father's brother) with him as Eddie also knew our 40 acres very well; they found the rifle under that windfall before dark, took it home and hid it in the back of a closet. The game warden searched our 40 all the next day in vain. Finally, at day's end, he came into our yard, perhaps to try to get my mother to give up the rifle. Instead, he was faced with a 5 ft. tall, 140 lb very irate woman. Before the warden could say anything, my mother lashed into him with some choice words. "You put my husband, the father of these little girls, in jail. Now who is going to chop wood for the stove?" She pointed to the woodshed and Mr. Smith knew what she meant. He headed directly to the woodshed, picked up the ax, and proceeded to chop wood.

This went on for several days, Mr. Smith looking for the rifle during most of the day and chopping wood for our mother before leaving. Finally he gave up on finding the rifle; probably he had even looked under the very windfall where it had initially been hidden. Our father was released from jail to the consternation of the warden.

I was born the following summer and 6 months later my father died in an automobile accident. His two prized possessions, that 30-40 Krag rifle and a mandolin, were presumed to be passed on to someone on his side of the family. I guess it was thought that my sisters would not be playing the mandolin and certainly they were not going to be hunting. Sure, I was a boy but only 6 months old and it would be over a decade before I would be hunting. Thus while I was told about the mandolin and the rifle, all the years of my youth and adulthood I had no idea of their whereabouts or whether either was still in existence.

In the summer of 2006, from out of the blue, my cousin Ben called my second youngest sister who lives about 5 miles from me. Neither my sister nor I had seen Ben for years and years. He said he and his wife were coming through our small town and wondered if we could all get together, which we did at a local restaurant the next morning. During breakfast I was showing Ben my first book, "Brook Trout and Uncle Willy," and we began talking about Uncle Willy, about other uncles and various hunting experiences. I said that soon I'd begin my second book, "Grouse, Deer, and Uncle Willy" and he immediately said, catching me by surprise, "You know, Jim, I have your father's rifle." Wow! I couldn't believe it. Could Ben be referring to that infamous rifle, hidden under the windfall by my father, then hidden by our grandfather and Uncle Eddie in their closet, and searched for but not found by the game warden? Might I finally see that rifle?

Ben said I could have the rifle but I'd have to come visit him to acquire it. He lives in a neighboring state and due to a variety of circumstances, it seemed unlikely that I would get there. I suggested he drop it off with Uncle Willy since Ben visits our home town now and then and Uncle Willy could then get it to me via a friend or relative coming my way. In Feb., 2007, my sister Lydia and her husband visited Uncle Willy to celebrate his 90th birthday. They invited Ben and his wife to join them, which they did, and Ben brought the rifle, the 30-40 Krag, Model 1898, manufactured by the U.S. Springfield Armory. As soon as Uncle Willy saw that rifle, he said to my sister, "this is definitely the rifle that your father hunted with and Jim will be happy to finally receive it after all these years." Pictures were taken when the rifle was transferred from Ben's hands to my sister Lydia's hands in our home town. Lydia packed the rifle into their car, wrapped in a carpet, and some weeks later my sister Phyllis and her husband Hank visited them and obtained the rifle. They delivered it to me with much excitement. Seeing that 30-40 Krag almost brought tears to my eyes. I believe that my father would have wanted me to have that rifle and from then on I was going to cherish it. If there is a Heaven and if my father is there, I would think he was pleased to be looking down on us and seeing me holding that rifle and smiling from ear to ear. Then we took more pictures of the transfer of the rifle into my hands. Note: The reader should be made aware that a portion of this story, written by my sister Lydia, appeared in The Sunday Sun, Nov. 27, 1977, Marquette, MI.

After telling Uncle Willy that I had obtained the long lost rifle from Cousin Ben, he remembered that my father had purchased the rifle from a Hunting and Trapping Company for $12.50. That was a lot of money back then and it is no wonder he hid it from the warden.

My brother-in-law Hank, a gun expert, provided me with some background information on this rifle. The 30-40 Krag was the first smoke-less powder repeater rifle to enter the U.S. Military service and was utilized by the U.S. Army. This was in the year 1892 and it was a Model 1892

30-40 Krag. The name Krag came about from the fact that the 30-40 was an improved version of the Danish Krag-Jorgensen Model of 1889. Later models 1896 and 1898 came forth. Interestingly, the Navy and Marine Corps never adopted the Krag, and the Army replaced it in 1903 by the far superior 30-06, a rifle much more familiar to hunters today.

A day after getting the rifle home, I got out my gun-cleaning equipment and began cleaning and lubricating it. The barrel was so filthy I must have pushed cleaning cloths through it over a hundred times, with intermittent runs of a wire brush, and then the wire brush with cloth wrapped around it, followed by more cloths, usually soaked in powder solvent. Finally, after some hours, the cloths began to come though reasonably clean. I concluded that the rifle had not been cleaned after the last person fired it. I pondered whether that person was my father or his brother.

The next thing on the agenda was to have Hank do an inspection of the rifle, as the 30-40 Krag rifles are known to develop cracks. He found none. I then purchased a box of cartridges and the two of us took it the firing range. The rifle has open sights which I was immediately comfortable with because the front sight fit so nicely within the rear sight. But unfortunately my first two shots from 50 yards were not accurate; I not only did not hit the one foot diameter target but did not hit the backup cardboard. I wondered at that point if the rifle was going to be so inaccurate that I could not hunt with it. Hank suggested we move the target closer, to 25 yards, and try it again. This time we noted that both bullets hit the cardboard above the target, but right in line with the bull's-eye. We adjusted the rear sight just slightly to bring the shot down and I fired two more times and both shots were right in the bull's-eye. We then moved the target back to 50 yards and now both of us were able to put several rounds in the bull's-eye. It did provide quite a "kick" and we used a shoulder cushion. Still, neither of us flinched. We did a "high five" and agreed it would be fine for hunting that coming season. I was excited because if I bagged a deer, I could say that I was a successful deer hunter with a rifle that my father had much success with eight decades previously.

    I was not able to hunt the first two days of season (2007) due to visiting an ailing sister. On the third day of season I was in my blind before the crack of dawn, the 30-40 Krag at the ready. However, not only did I not see a deer but I didn't see a deer that I had a good shot at all season. The only deer I saw were one's I spooked up from thickets and a shot would have been worthless to try. I knew there were deer in or passing through my 40 because the bait was eaten during the night and, after a light snow fall on the fifth day of season, there were plenty of tracks. I puzzled over the fact that the deer had become so nocturnal. Finally I reasoned that it was because I had loggers there from Sept. to just before deer hunting season. The loggers were clear-cutting five 50 yard-wide by 200 yard long swaths of mainly cedar and white pine forest that had formed a complete canopy, my idea being to get new growth to come in to provide food and cover for wildlife and song birds. Somehow this logging activity, perhaps the chain saws and/or the large skidder machine, caused the deer to change their behavior from the year before. The puzzle was that while the loggers were there the deer moved freely to downed trees to browse, even in the day time. I was skunked and could not bag a deer with my father's rifle. All I could do was look forward to the next season and with the clear-cut zones growing in somewhat already, I thought there might be even more deer than usual on the 40. My plan was to have that rifle zeroed in for 100 yards as I am quite certain it will be accurate at that distance. Then, according to the view of Hank, I could adjust for 150 yards and 50 yards easily. Now I'm looking forward to taking that 30-40 Krag to the range again, with Hank along of course.

During our visit to obtain the rifle, Lydia asked, "don't most hunters have a 22 for hunting varmints and also a shotgun for hunting grouse and rabbits?" When that question was raised to Uncle Willy he agreed that my father had those guns but had no idea where they might be. Maybe some day I will set out on a search through the family for those guns. Each is probably standing behind a closet door of another of my cousin's. Now I'm contemplating how to begin that search.

Ben insisted he only had the 30-40 Krag and no shotgun or 22. However, a few weeks after I had cleaned that Krag and we had fired it at the range, I sent an e-mail to Ben with a progress report. Amazingly, he wrote back and said, "You know, Jim, I have your dad's mandolin too." Wow! What a surprise. Well, I then acquired the mandolin with the help of my sisters Edna and Lydia and their husbands. What an amazing thing to see that long lost mandolin. I immediately searched out a mandolin expert who repaired a broken string and tuned the instrument. Then a friend gave me a book with a CD and a DVD on "How To Play The Mandolin" and I have begun to learn to play. I'm experiencing many of life's small pleasures.

This past deer hunting season, 2008, I had both my 77 Ruger with a telescopic sight and the 30-40 Krag in my deer blind. Baiting was illegal due to the danger of spreading disease from deer to deer via saliva but I nevertheless saw an abundance of deer both from my blind and while walking and posting around my 40. Deer learned to walk through the forested areas just inside the edge of the clear cut openings – a funneling effect. One afternoon from the window of my blind I watched a large doe and a smaller antlerless deer bed down at noon next to some brush left from the loggers. They would occasionally get up and stretch, browse for a few minutes, and then bed down again, finally leaving at 4:30 PM. Still, sometimes deer could be seen right in the middle of the clear-cut areas. My plan was to use the Ruger with 308 cartridges for any shots of over 50 yards as I was still not confident with the Krag at farther distances. It was not the fault of the rifle but of my eyes and trifocal eye glasses, especially with open sights. If I had a shot closer than 50 yards I would use the Krag. Well, I did get a shot with the Ruger at a 6 point buck but it was at about 90 yards and I only wounded it. After trailing it through 4 adjacent 40's of private land and then to where it had crossed my crick heading into still more private land, it was near dark and I had to give up the trail until morning. After a light snowfall, in the morning I resumed tracking it, finding specks of blood here and there, and then I spooked it off its bed. While there was some blood on the bed, I lost the trail in that thicket due to the many and varied deer tracks. My hope was that it survived and perhaps it did because days later, looking north from my blind window, I observed a buck chasing a doe, both running full tilt, but I did not get a shot. I thought it might be that same buck. Near the end of season I used the Ruger to fill my antlerless tag. The shot was from about 80 yards and the deer dropped on the spot. Thus there was nothing wrong with the accuracy of the Ruger so I don't know why I missed that buck earlier. Perhaps the cartridge was deflected by a branch.

Now I am waiting for the season of 2009 to perhaps finally shoot a buck with my father's 30-40 Krag. I'll have it zeroed in for 100 yards and just need to be confident to take that long shot. Maybe that buck I wounded last season will still be visiting my 40 and be a 6 or 8 pointer by then.

Chapter Ten
Uncles and Violating.

I first realized my uncles violated when I was 12 and playing hide and seek in the hay barn with my buddies one afternoon. It was mid-December and the temperature was in the low 20's, with several feet of snow on the ground. The hay barn was not heated so it was just about as cold as the ambient temperature outside. I went to hide under the hay and felt something that was not hay. Digging the hay off, I came upon the frozen carcass of an antlerless deer. I thought of calling my buddies over to see it but decided that the deer had been shot illegally and I probably should not tell anyone. I covered it back up with hay and went on playing hide and seek. Later I mentioned the deer to my mother, whispering so no one else would know I had discovered it. She said, "Your Uncle Ned shot it two days ago at his place and he thought it would be better to hide it here on the farm and process it here." She said it in sort of a matter-of-fact way, as if it was not an uncommon event.

Two falls later, when I was 14, I was able to buy a license and hunt for the first time. After we got home from hunting on the second day of season, Nov. 16, Uncle Ned drove into the farm yard. He talked quietly with Uncle Willy and my grandfather. Uncle Willy then told me Uncle Ned had shot a doe, which was an illegal deer back then, over by Black Crick, and that we would drag it out later that night. Well, later turned out to be 9 PM, my bed time. My two uncles and I drove to the old logging road leading to Black Crick, with which we were all familiar. We took rope and flashlights and headed east along the old road, Uncle Ned in the lead and me last. Uncle Ned instructed us to not use a flashlight unless absolutely necessary. There was a full moon so most of the time we didn't need flashlights. Ned was very paranoid – maybe thinking the game warden might be out there in the woods waiting for us, or in the air in a small plane looking down. His paranoia apparently served him well as Uncle Willy could not recall his brother ever getting caught violating.

We walked for at least 45 minutes, huffing and puffing, stumbling along sometimes in the dark when trees shaded the moonlight. Fortunately the terrain was mostly flat until the last several hundred yards heading into the crick valley. I had walked this old logging road many times the previous winter while checking my weasel traps but that was on snowshoes and in daylight. Finally we stopped and Uncle Ned whispered that the deer was in there, about 25 yards, and he pointed to the right. We then used one flashlight and walked into the woods. Sure enough, there was the doe, hidden under a windfall. Uncle Willy tied the front legs to the head and then the rope was looped around the front legs and the neck so that the deer was pulled head-end first, "with the grain" of the hide. Uncle Willy reminded me that the hair on a deer's hide slants toward its rear end and if you pulled it by the back feet first, it would be pulled against the grain. Taking turns, two of us pulling at a time,

Grouse, Deer, and Uncle Willy

we dragged that deer along the dark road for over an hour finally reaching Uncle Ned's car and we loaded it into the trunk. Uncle Willy, breathing hard, then said, to Uncle Ned, only half-kiddingly, "Next time, shoot the doe a little closer to civilization." Uncle Ned mumbled something I couldn't understand and then said, "It will be good meat."

Dragging an illegal deer out of the woods in near darkness is not fun. *Uncle Willy and Jim drag the deer that Uncle Ned illegally shot miles from civilization. Uncle Ned scarcely shows any light on the old logging road with his flashlight, being afraid the game warden will see the light and come arrest them. Uncle Willy scolded him, not for shooting an illegal deer, but for shooting one so far in the deep woods.*

The propensity of my Uncles and Grandfather to violate was further demonstrated to me one Thanksgiving day.

Typically, by Thanksgiving we had over 2 feet of snow and this year was no exception. Uncle Willy, my grandfather, and I drove to what was called Moran's swamp, a very good blueberry picking area in the summer. It was a huge area with only a few homes scattered here and there. I wondered why anyone would live so far in the "boon docks" and I still wonder the same today when I see homes so far removed from civilization. We hunted for a few hours but no one saw deer. There was fresh snow, more was coming down, and the forest was beautiful but we had to head back to the farm for Thanksgiving dinner. As we began to empty our rifles at the car, a deer appeared on the old one lane road, at least a hundred and fifty yards away. With the light snow falling it was impossible to determine if it was a buck or doe. My grandfather apparently did not care either way as he set his long-barreled 30-30 on top of the already opened car door, took aim, and fired. The deer ran into the woods, a clean miss it seemed as we found no trace of blood when we drove up to the spot and examined the tracks. My grandfather acknowledged that it was a difficult shot.

A third time I witnessed a case of violating was late one season when I was making a deer drive towards the posters, Uncle Willy and Uncle Karl. Now that I think of it, I never remember anyone driving deer towards me as a poster; I was always the driver. Anyway, a snowfall had occurred the previous night and a beautiful blanket of white snow covered everything. After about 20 minutes into my drive going north, I heard a shot in front of me. After another 15 minutes or so I came out on the two track my two uncles were posting on. There was Uncle Karl, smoking a cigarette, standing under an evergreen and sporting the biggest guilty grin I'd ever seen. We used to call that kind of grin a "shit eating" grin and to this day I don't know why. As I approached Karl I noted blood all over that fresh snow. He had shot a doe, quickly dressed it, and had it hidden under a small hemlock tree. I shook my head because if a warden had come along there would have been no question about a deer having been shot on that spot. It would have been only a few minutes before the warden would have located that doe. The good thing about that case of violating was that the doe was not far from the main road and it did not take much effort for Uncle Karl, Uncle Willy, and me to drag it out of there that night.

While writing this chapter I could not recall a single instance wherein Uncle Willy shot an illegal deer. When I asked him about this, he admitted to following the game rules as close as he could. He did not deny violating but I gathered that he did not make a habit of it, like his brother Ned did.

As I began high school and certainly during my college years, I became conservation-minded. That stands to reason as I majored in biology and minored in conservation. This conservation attitude must have become noticeable during evening conversations during the summer or when I was home from college during holidays. I realized this fact because my grandfather and uncles told me less and less about shooting deer illegally until finally they never told me anything at all. Perhaps they thought it would bother me to know they violated. Or, worse yet, they might have thought I would report them to the warden. Neither was the case, of course, but nevertheless I am certain their violating exploits continued. I was just not made aware of them.

Another story about my uncles violating was passed on to me by Cousin Ric while we were having a phone conversation about Sparky and grouse hunting. I asked Ric whether his dad Ralph violated and he said, "yes." "Did he ever get caught?" I asked. "Yes, he did," answered Ric and he related this story. Ralph and Ric's mother had been berry picking north of their small farm in late summer. Even though small game season had not yet opened, Ralph had taken a single shot 22 rifle along, always being ready in case a game animal showed up. On the way back home, while walking along the old logging road, they looked up ahead and saw two men in green uniforms. "Game wardens," said Ralph, and he tossed the loaded 22 into the bushes. The wardens approached and asked Ralph why he was carrying a rifle before small game season opened. Ralph said, "I don't have a rifle." The wardens had seen him throw the rifle into the bushes and as they walked in to find it, Ralph took off running and didn't stop until he got home. Whatever the strategy for running was, it didn't work as the wardens showed up with Ric's mother about 30 minutes later, arrested Ralph, and took him downtown to jail. This infuriated Ric's mother and later that day she had a friend drive her into town, went to the jail, and let everyone know in no pleasant terms that Ralph was needed at home to milk the cows. He was immediately released.

When Ric told me this story, I realized how similar it was to the story about my father and the 30-40 Krag rifle (see Chapter 9). Could both stories be true? Was one story generated from the other? Were they both untrue? I called Uncle Willy and he said, "Yes, they are both true but they happened in different years." Then he added details to the story about his brother Ralph, indicating to me that it was in fact a true story. He also confirmed that the story about the arrest of my father was true.

There was a limit to the degree of violating Ralph would tolerate. One deer season, younger brother Karl was hunting with Ralph. Karl shot three antlerless deer, within minutes of each other, and received a severe scolding from his older brother Ralph. Still, all the meat was utilized and their father (my grandfather) had nothing negative to say.

A cruel form of violating was related to me by Uncle Willy. He and Ralph were hunting and came upon a small buck which was jumping and running around in small circles. The men wondered why the buck did not run off and thought it might be diseased. As they approached, they realized it was caught by the neck in a wire snare. They shot the buck, field dressed it, and took down the snare. Uncle Willy could not recall if they reported the snaring to the game warden.

Chapter Eleven
My First and Second Bucks

The hunting season I was 16 was my third season of hunting and not only had I not yet bagged a buck but I had not seen one. Oh I had seen plenty of antlerless deer the previous two seasons but not one single set of antlers. On this opening morning I was naturally excited and very determined that it was the year I was going to bag my first buck. My buddy Matt picked me up with his dad's 4 wheel drive jeep truck before the crack of dawn and we drove to what was mining company forest. There was no snow and it was about 40 degrees. We parked the truck, loaded our rifles; I had a lever action, open-sighted Winchester 30-30, Matt had his dad's 30-40 Krag. (Matt told me recently he regrets that his dad sold that old Krag for just a few dollars). We took a compass reading and noted the light wind was from the southwest. So we walked south about 200 yards directly perpendicular to the old two track logging road we had driven in on. It was just getting light. We separated by about 200 yards so we could just see each other and we each found a log to sit on looking towards the south and thus downwind from any deer. We had agreed to post there for two hours and then walk to the truck and decide what our next strategy would be. Sitting still for two hours was going to be much easier for Matt than for me and I was hoping a buck would come along quickly. Fortunately one did.

After about 30 minutes, I saw 3 deer walking slowly toward me, oblivious of my presence. As the 3 deer began walking past me on my left side, about 50 yards away, I noticed that the largest one was a buck as I could now clearly see antlers, even though it was a small rack. My heart was racing so fast I thought that buck, now my only concern, was going to hear it beating. I asked myself if buck fever was setting into my system. I turned and slowly lifted my rifle but as I did the log under me gave way and made a cracking sound which the deer heard. Before I could get a shot off, they bounded north toward the logging road. Then the buck stopped but the angle for a shot was not good and I could only see a little of its left shoulder past its rump. Still, I wanted that buck. So I aimed just past the left rump hoping to send a bullet into the left shoulder and if deep enough then into the heart. The buck dropped after I shot but immediately jumped up and ran off into a thicket before I could get another shot off.

Matt heard my shot and walked over to where I was. I quickly explained what had happened and we walked to where the buck had fallen. Sure enough there was an abundance of blood so it was apparent I had hit it well. Instead of waiting for the wounded buck to lie down, as is recommended, Matt and I excitedly started after it, easily following the blood trail, even without snow. About 100 yards ahead of us the buck was in fact lying down and as we approached it jumped up and dashed through some evergreens. There was no chance for a shot. Again being impatient we continued after the deer and after about 5 minutes we heard 3 shots just up ahead of us. Continuing and still following the blood trail, we saw another hunter stooped over the buck, a nice five pointer, now lying dead. The man was putting his tag on an antler. We walked up to him and I nervously said, "I shot this buck back there and it is rightfully my deer. Look at the blood trail. It would not have survived for long." The man was about 30 yrs old and bigger than either of us. He answered, "No way. That deer was running full speed and it came from over there," and he pointed to the north. I looked at Matt disappointed as all get out and we nodded to each other to leave. We walked back to his truck, both dejected to not have that buck. It was a big, healthy deer. We discussed the situation together and then I discussed it a few days later with Uncle Willy. We all agreed that the deer was certainly the one I had shot at and hit and that it was a fatal wound, but we concluded there was nothing we could do. If only I had waited patiently after that first shot before trailing it I could have had my buck. But, Matt and I were both encouraged by everyone to keep trying.

 The next morning, the second day of season, I went out hunting with another buddy, Ron, and we went to another area of the same mining company forest. We left my house before daybreak with a thermos of hot coffee and some of my mother's donuts. Ron drove in as far as we dared to on an old logging road and parked the car on the side in a dry spot. We each got our rifle out, closed the car doors as quietly as possible, loaded up, checked the safety, took a compass reading, and walked in along the old road another 150 yards or so. The forest was good deer country being a mixture of aspen of various sizes, with some evergreens and maples. I had my 30-30 Winchester and Ron was using his Dad's 30-06. Again, with a light SW wind as on opening day, we walked south into the forest about 200 yards, splitting up as we walked, and we both posted. I sat on an old log that was against an aspen so I had a backrest. Ron was to my right about 150 yards away but I could not see him after he sat in his posting position, also facing south.

As on the previous day, again after about 30 minutes of posting and it now being fully light, I noted a single deer walking slowly through an aspen thicket, heading right between Ron and me but closer to me. As it got between us, I could see it had antlers but the rack was not large. I thought to myself that this deer resembled the one I "almost" bagged yesterday. I raised my rifle but before cocking the hammer back, I thought of Ron possibly being directly in the line of fire. So I let the buck get considerably past the point where Ron would be in the line of fire. Fortunately it stopped and looked right at me for a few moments, then it looked straight ahead in the direction it was walking. I drew a bead just behind its right shoulder and pulled the trigger. The buck jumped and began high-tailing toward the old logging road. At the very moment it jumped Ron began firing, bang, bang, bang. I levered another cartridge into the chamber but I did not fire again, being confident I had hit it in a vital spot the first time. And, although I was following the buck with my sights, there was no really good shot available. The buck ran about 75 yards and dropped. Both Ron and I reached the buck at the same time. Ron said, "I had just taken aim at that buck when you shot. When it took off running I thought maybe you had missed it so I started shooting."

Jim's second buck. *When Jim first saw this 4 pt buck it was right between him and Ron so he could not shoot. The buck fortunately walked 30 yards to the north and gave Jim a safe shot. It was the second buck Jim shot but the first one he tagged. Ron field-dressed it, and together they dragged it to Ron's car.*

When we excitedly examined the buck, which was a 4 pointer, indeed my bullet had entered the buck behind its right shoulder and interestingly had lodged just under the skin of the left side. It was as if the bullet ran out of energy just as it passed through the rib cage and stopped before passing through the skin on the opposite side. Ron kidded me that it was his bullet under the skin. However, I reminded him that if it was his, it would have been lodged under the skin of the buck's right side. Ron had apparently missed with all 3 shots but the deer had been running full speed. We field dressed the deer together, with Ron doing most of the hard part and getting the most bloodied-up. The bullet had nicked the heart and done much damage to the lungs so the chest cavity was filled with blood. We had brought a short piece of rope which we tied around the buck's antlers and front feet and then dragged the buck to Ron's car and lifted it into the trunk. We headed right to my house, unloaded the deer, and hoisted it up by the back legs in the hay barn, where Uncle Willy, my mother, stepfather, and I processed it three days later. We made sure Ron's family received some choice cuts.

Matt got skunked that season but Ron bagged his buck, a large 8 pointer, on the fourth day of the season while hunting with his brother Tony. Just as he always outdid me when brook trout fishing, catching more and larger trout, he outdid me while deer hunting. Ron now has a hunting camp near Black Crick and rarely does a season go by when he does not bag a buck.

Chapter Twelve
Musings in a Deer Blind

When Uncle Willy first took me deer hunting, we did not have a blind nor, to my knowledge, did anyone else. We would find a likely place to see deer, usually a runway, and sit or stand and wait (posting) for the deer to come by, then walk some, and again post. The length of each posting period was determined by the hunter's patience and the temperature of his/her feet. Baiting was not legal and never once occurred to me as a means of attracting deer. In my mind, deer ate browse and nothing but browse. Now, 5-6 decades later, most hunters use a blind and they add bait (corn, carrots, apples, and/or sugar beets) to attract the deer. I hunt both ways, from a blind with a bait pile but also walking and posting. However, because of the fear of spreading disease from deer to deer, baiting was made illegal for the 2008 season. I still used the blind but spent more time walking, stalking, and posting which I really enjoyed. The baiting ban will be continued through the 2009 season.

My deer blind has windows on all sides so that I can observe in all directions. Usually I only look south, west, and north as the wind is generally from one of those directions.

In the rare case of an east wind, I will swivel my chair and look north, east, and south. My blind is on a knoll and thus I am looking down ever so slightly. There is low land to the south with a brook trout crick running through it. I have seen deer approach from all 4 directions but most often they arrive to my bait pile from the low land, coming from the southwest.

When sitting quietly in a deer blind, whether at the crack of dawn, mid-day, or near sunset, there is always activity. Non-hunters often ask, "How can you sit in that blind all day long? Don't you get bored?" Well, there may be some moments of boredom but I for one have not experienced many. For one thing, while it is most exciting to see deer it is also exciting to be prepared and ready to bag a deer from the blind. The anticipation is a constant thing. It is important to continually survey the forest for deer, ideally with binoculars. There are many other animals to be seen, namely birds and small mammals, and you see some unusual events. For example, I witnessed a hawk dive bomb down and pick off a blue jay off my bait pile. Finally, I've known hunters who do wood carving, reading, or even studying a foreign language while in the blind, not to mention napping. I've done all but the wood carving.

Just as it is getting light, having sat in the blind for at least an hour already, the first animal sound I hear is the clucking of turkeys as these large game birds drop from their roost and begin to forage. The sound is from the lowland down near the crick. Next I hear the chatter of a red squirrel, next blue jays, then chickadees, almost always in that order. Soon after I hear these animals, they can be sighted, although turkeys often do not appear. Grouse will visit the bait pile in the early morning and late in the afternoon. Red squirrels, gray squirrels, blue jays, and chickadees are regular visitors, present all day. An occasional opossum will saunter along, sometimes visiting the bait pile, and I've seen red fox on occasion but not at the bait pile. Crows and hawks are often present but never directly at the bait pile. While in my blind I have not seen a raccoon, mink, weasel, badger, coyote, or owl but I have seen them at other times on my 40 acres.

Sometimes a deer or several deer can be very predictable and appear at a certain time in the morning, daytime, or evening, and can be recognized after a few visits. Two seasons ago I had a button buck visiting every day, always about 8:30 AM, coming from the NW, but only for the first week of the season. Did someone shoot it? One season a doe showed up on a regular basis with two almost grown-up fawns, the young ones being quite frisky and not wary, whereas the mother was fidgety and very wary, her tail often flashing white and her front foot stomping the ground. Perhaps she was catching a human scent, no doubt mine from being careless when adding bait. One fall before the season opened I sat in the blind for 4 evenings until dark and a nice 5 point buck visited every evening, taking its time eating corn and apples. When the season opened, I never saw that buck again.

With all these animals visiting the bait pile, I began to sort out a hierarchy of dominance. One would think deer would be dominant and then one could go down in size to the smallest animals. Not so exactly. Red squirrels dominated over blue jays and blue jays over chickadees. Opossums dominated over red squirrels and grouse but grouse were dominant to red squirrels. I ranked red and gray squirrels very close but would give the smaller red a slight nod over the larger gray (and its black variation). I never got a chance to see an opossum at the same time as a wild turkey but one might guess the opossum might be dominant. What surprised me one morning was to see the doe and her two young ones at the bait pile, eating contentedly, when approximately 25 turkeys came marching into view, led by a hen, and headed right for the bait pile. The deer all spooked and ran off, leaving the turkeys to clean up the corn. I wondered if the deer would have acted like they did if only one or two turkeys had showed up. And what if a buck had been at the bait pile? Would it have gotten spooked off? I've not seen such an interaction again so have only the one observation. Given these limited observations (anecdotal data) I would make the dominance hierarchy order, lowest to highest, as follows: chickadee, blue jay, gray squirrel, red squirrel, grouse, opossum, deer, and wild turkey.

Red squirrels are fascinating as stashers. They will carry off corn kernels very long distances (at least 50 yards I estimated), following basically the same route each time, and then come back to the bait pile along a slightly different route. Finally, after a dozen trips or so, they will take a new route in a new direction and make that trip a dozen times, then another route, and another route, all day long. How many kernels they carry off each time I have no way of knowing. Nor did I know how many the busy squirrel had to eat during the day to provide the energy to make those long trips. Obviously there was an energy gain otherwise it would seem the squirrels would only make short trips. One can argue benefits for squirrels having several stashes, in case another squirrel or blue jay robs one or more of them (see below).

The fall of 2006 I added some acorns to the bait pile which I had raked up in our yard from under our many oak trees. Note that our house is in a small village, about 5 miles from our farm. There being no oaks on our farm, I thought the acorns (mast) would attract deer. Acorns attracted all right but primarily red squirrels and to a lesser extent gray squirrels. This time the stash sight was not so far, and one day a busy red squirrel made 11 trips to stash acorns under some leaves on the side of a small hill. I assumed it was carrying one acorn at a time. Then it started a new route and continued stashing there, followed by still another route and another stash, each with 9-12 acorns, this behavior continuing all morning. What surprised me was that the squirrel began to rummage in the first stash site and I thought it was going to add to it. No, instead it dug up all those acorns and moved them another 10 yards farther into still another stash site. What possessed it to make this move I had no idea at the time. I wondered how often squirrels move stashed food to another site and why they do it. In this regard, a study was reported by Molly Newman on gray squirrels titled "Baffling the Bandits" (National Wildlife, 2008). Apparently moving stashes is to lead "pilferers" astray, meaning other squirrels and bluejays.. Just when a thief thinks he/she knows where the "money" is, it is moved to another site. Gray squirrels will also dig a hole and cover over it without putting the acorn into it. Then it moves to another hole and buries it there. How does this anti-pilfering behavior come about? Is it learned? My observations indicate that red squirrels have also developed this anti-pilfering behavior.

Squirrels love corn, including that which was still on the cob. While in his blind, brother-in-law Hank described a corn cob moving along the ground, bump, bump, bump, one early morning, only to see when he looked through his binoculars that a red squirrel was tugging it along. After the few times I added cobbed corn to my bait pile, I would find cleaned cobs a long distance from the bait pile, sometimes more than 50 yards away.

Squirrels will also eat apples. They will sometimes gnaw on apples at the bait pile but they will also carry off apples to their stash. Once I heard a noise from just outside my blind as if a heavy object fell out of a tree. When I left the blind later I curiously checked to see what that object was and found it to be an apple. I thought, "squirrels are amazing to be able to haul a rather large apple up a tree." Then I actually witnessed just that, and the squirrel left the apple precariously positioned on some branches, about 25 ft above ground. Sure enough, after an hour or so, the apple crashed to the ground. One wonders what goes through a squirrel's mind when dealing with an apple.

Blue jays are also stashers. From the number of times they peck down into the corn, I could estimate how many kernels they pick up, assuming one kernel for each peck. The range I counted was 5-9. The blue jay would then fly off, anywhere from 2 yards away to so far that the bird would be out of sight, perhaps up to 100 yards. Again, one wonders about the energy pay off. As with squirrels, the blue jays used more than one stash site, in fact, they seemed to never place more than those 5-9 kernels in any one stash site. Their stash site was always in trees and never on the ground.

One day I began to count the number of corn kernels carried off by squirrels and blue jays, ignoring what chickadees take. Calculating the time between trips, from

15 to 35 seconds for blue jays and from 10 to 45 seconds for squirrels, and knowing the average number of kernels taken each time (1 for squirrels and 7 for blue jays), one can see how 2 gallons of corn kernels can disappear during the course of a day without a single deer visiting the bait pile. Now if one adds what 25 wild turkeys might take, the corn is gone rather quickly. Furthermore, grouse and opossums also take corn.

Grouse have a crop for food storage. After bagging my first grouse while hunting with Uncle Willy, he showed me that the crop was loaded with clover. Whatever a grouse eats, be it a mixture of seeds and clover or aspen buds, it first goes into the crop for temporary storage. Now, sitting in my blind, I wondered how many corn kernels a grouse could pack into its crop. That number was arrived at by counting the number of pecks a grouse made at the bait pile before it sauntered away into the thicket. Assuming one kernel per peck at the corn, and observing two grouse on two separate days, I counted 34 and 37. That is a large number of kernels and seemingly would provide enough energy to last the grouse for some days. Interestingly, the many grouse I observed always walked up to the bait pile with one exception. Once a grouse did come flying in. I never saw more than two grouse at the same time. More than once I flushed a grouse from the bait pile as I approached. Of course I could have been observing the same two grouse each day. On occasion a grouse will peck at an apple for many minutes, taking away a good portion.

Deer are most fascinating to watch at the bait pile Some deer will be very spooky and hardly dare to approach. Other deer will have absolutely no fear and casually approach and stand there eating and eating, only occasionally looking around, sometimes directly towards my blind window. Deer will sometimes be seen approaching from a long distance away. Other times they appear like apparitions and are there at the bait pile suddenly. Was I napping or just not paying attention? Before day break deer will appear as ghostly shapes, moving around the bait pile, as I study the heads with my binoculars trying to see if antlers are present. Sometimes those deer are gone by the time enough light arrives to make a determination. The same phenomenon can be seen in the evening. As the season progresses, the deer visit the bait pile later and later in the evening until one has to really strain to see them, by then it being impossible to see antlers and too late to legally shoot one anyway. The largest number of deer I've seen at one time at the bait pile has been 5. Not all deer passing by visit the bait pile and those deer, if I cannot see the head clearly, I usually suspect are bucks. The largest number of deer I've seen on any single day of hunting season was 12, but of course some of those were likely the same deer. As I mention in the following chapter, I concluded by observing tracks in fresh snow that 9 deer had passed into or passed through my 40 acres during one night.

One morning looking down the old road heading into the low land, I observed an unusual animal down near the crick, about 200 yards away. It was so early there was barely enough light to see it. I didn't see it approach but there it was, standing very still, positioned with its left side toward me. Its head was small, it had a bump on its neck, its body was long and deep, and its legs were short and spindly. I wondered what this strange-looking animal was and where it came from. My first thought was that it was a musk ox, perhaps an escapee from the dairy farm next door. Would they have a musk ox? That seemed unlikely. I also considered that it was a strange dog but its shape hardly resembled that of a dog. I held my binoculars on the animal for what seemed like a long time but it was probably no more than 5-10 minutes. During this time it was slowly getting lighter. All of sudden the shape of the animal began to change, lengthened even more, and the bump on the neck changed positions. Ha! I laughed as I realized what it was – two deer silhouetted, standing sideways, one slightly advanced. They stood there so very still for a long time while I was visualizing a musk ox. Perhaps they were looking at something ahead of them or looking toward my blind. A picture would have been great but it would have required infrared photography. Those two deer finally wondered off down the crick without showing any interest in coming up the road to my bait pile. With farms on two sides and an abundance of corn and alfalfa, not to mention additional bait piles of other hunters, my small bait pile was likely a low priority.

GROUSE, DEER, AND UNCLE WILLY

A strange beast is down by the crick. (A) Looking down toward the crick as it was just getting light, Jim saw an odd-looking animal, sort of like a musk ox. It had a hump and many short legs. What was it? The strange animal stood there for maybe 10 minutes, while daylight improved. (B) Jim realized what the strange beast was as one deer finally walked forward of the second deer behind it. (C) It was two deer standing next to

James Woodsing

each other, sort of silhouetted, but they could not be distinguished in the darkness of early morning.

Most deer hunters have seen deer approach and when the deer sees them, as still as the hunter might stand or sit, the deer realizes the hunter does not "fit" into the landscape. A deer will stand absolutely still and look directly at the hunter for a long time. One day I left my blind and walked down to the crick and posted between the trunks of three large white pines. After about 10 minutes, I witnessed a button buck looking at me from across the crick. How long had it been there I wondered? It did not move so much as an ear for 15 minutes while it continued to stare at me. It was painful for me to stand still for that long a time but I finally out-lasted that little buck and it moved off, still wary and still occasionally looking at me.

Chapter Thirteen
Counting Deer: Tracks after a Snow Fall

One of life's small pleasures in retirement is to be able to hunt grouse and deer. I restrict my hunting almost entirely to our 40 acre "farm" up north, a most interesting piece of property that is divided into high land on the north and south sides and a low land area in between with a small brook trout crick meandering through it. There are cedar, white and red pine, hemlock, aspen, birch, maple, apple, and cherry trees. The clear areas that existed when we purchased the property (see My Own Trout Stream, in: "Brook Trout and Uncle Willy") now are filling in with red pine, white pine, spruce and apple trees, from 5 to 20 ft high, that my wife, daughter, friends, and I have planted through the 15 years we have owned the property. It is surrounded by a farm field to the north which is usually planted in alfalfa, forest on the other three sides, and there is a large dairy farm just to the southwest adjacent to the crick just before it enters our property. More alfalfa fields are on the farm proper.

Based on observations of beds, buck rubs and scrapes, and the numerous sightings of deer all year long, I knew there were many deer that passed through this 40 acres and possibly some that spent most of their time within the property. Certainly one of the main food sources in the absence of snow was the alfalfa field to the north. More than one evening, before hunting season opened, I watched deer come out of the area with red pine plantings, leap the barbed wire fence, and commence feeding on the alfalfa. Water is available from two vernal ponds through June and from the crick all year.

I had been curious for a long time as to just how many deer come and go through our 40 acre property and how many actually reside within the property. I had the chance to obtain data relevant to these questions one morning during the 2004 deer hunting season. After the first week of the season I had not yet seen a deer with antlers. As I was leaving the farm at dusk on the seventh day, I thought back to the half dozen or so antlerless deer I had seen that day. It had begun snowing as I was leaving my blind and by the time I unloaded my rifle and cased it and got out of my orange hunting vest at my truck, parked at the property entrance, the snow was coming down quite heavily. It occurred to me that the following morning was going to be great hunting as the ground was going to be white and deer tracks would be readily visible.

The conditions couldn't have been more perfect. The snowfall ended some time before daybreak and when I reached the farm at 6:30 AM, about a half hour before daybreak, everything was covered with a beautiful white coating of soft snow, about 5 inches deep. As I walked back to my blind, I could see deer tracks made at different times during the snow fall. Some were well-covered, some barely-covered, and some were fresh, indicating that deer had moved through the property at different times during the night. The question I asked was, "How many deer were in my property last night?" The fact that sometimes the tracks indicated 1 deer, sometimes 2 and other times 3 deer would argue for different deer but couldn't rule out the same 3 deer; they could have merely split up into a pair and a single.

Most interesting were the "fresh" tracks, those without newly fallen snow covering them. These I wanted to examine but I needed to wait until daylight. There were so many tracks around my bait pile it looked like the deer had had a party and I could see that those tracks would take some time to sort out. I sat in my blind until daylight was full, about 7:30 AM. No deer showed up, not even the one button buck that had routinely been coming by. I decided to do the "track" study and left the blind to collect data. I didn't have paper and pencil so everything was going to have to be mentally recorded. First I examined the tracks coming and going from the bait pile area. Three deer had come up from the lowland so I followed their tracks backwards to where they had leaped over the crick, and then continued following them backwards to where they entered our 40 from the forest to the south. Then I came back to the bait pile area and followed a set of 3 tracks away from the bait pile going east. Near the east edge of my 40, I spooked five deer off their beds near a thicket of evergreens. To be sure of the number I counted the beds and there were in fact five. The only one I got a good look at was antler-less. All five leaped over the fence and headed into the forest to the east. These five deer were clearly within the property and likely would have stayed on their beds through a good part of the day. Following the tracks backwards to the bait pile, I noted that two deer had veered to the north from the bait pile and then met the three whose tracks I followed directly to the bedding location.

From there I headed north along the fence bordering the property and then west, continuing to walk the periphery of the entire 40. I would make a mental note from the tracks as to how many deer came into the property and how many left the property. Two deer left and walked north through the alfalfa field, heading to the forest on the north side of the field. Farther along going west along the fence, I noted that no deer entered the property from the north. However, four deer in two pairs entered the property from the west, coming from across the road, and three from the southwest. Finally, two additional deer entered the property from the south and leaped the crick, about 150 yards upstream from the bridge where I had seen the musk ox (see Chapter 12). Thus I encircled the entire property, stopping to follow tracks into or leaving the property, which took the better part of three hours. After a coffee break at my blind, I then did some more walking through the middle sections of the property, further examining tracks and looking for beds. There were tracks consistent with my observations about deer entering and leaving the property but I found no additional beds. From examining tracks in this way, I concluded that at least nine different deer had been within our 40 acres during that night and that five of them were bedded down within the property that morning. Of course this night could have been exceptional and that number might have been less than usual or more than usual.

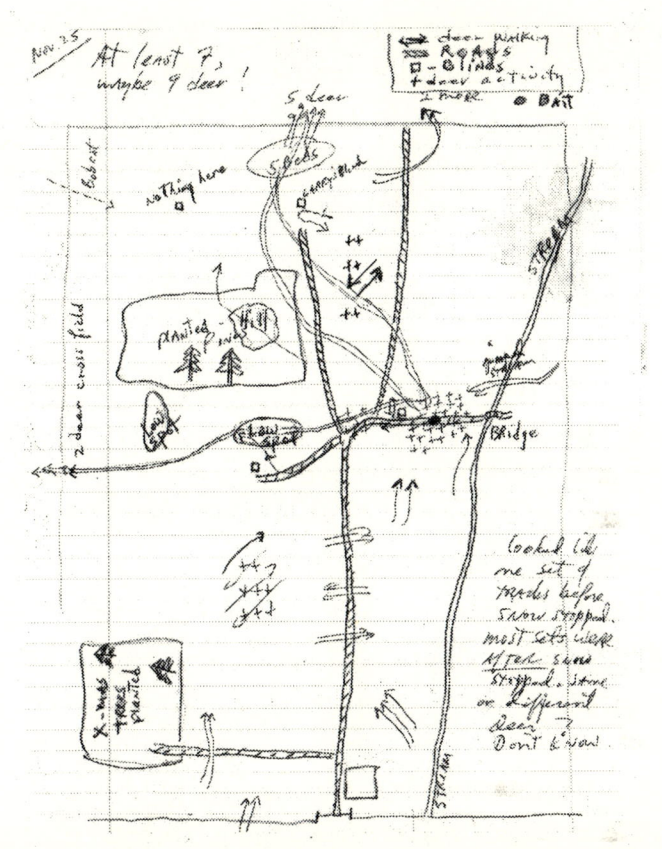

Jim estimated the number of deer in his 40 acres by constructing a map of the fresh deer tracks after a snow fall the night before. It had started snowing in the evening and continued all night, finally stopping a few hrs before dawn. Thus it was possible to separate "old" from "fresh" tracks. By walking the perimeter of the 40 acres, and walking back and forth within the property, the number of deer that had come into and left the property could be determined. Jim concluded that 9 deer had been within the property during the early morning hours, after the snow stopped falling, 5 of which were bedded down within the property.

It was disappointing that in '05, '06, '07, and the most recent hunting season, '08, while hunting with my father's 30-40 Krag (see Chapter 9), we did not have a favorable snowfall. Thus I have not been able to repeat this study. What I can say from examining tracks on the property after several different light snow falls is that there were numerous deer passing into and through the property and several bedded down within the property during the day. Also, in different seasons, I have often spooked deer within the property, sometimes from their beds. Perhaps some subsequent fall there will be an ideal snow fall for another tracking study. Furthermore, it would now be particularly interesting given that I had 5 large areas clear-cut in 2007-2008. In fact, determining the number of deer will be of interest in subsequent years as the clear-cut areas fill in with growth. In the winter months of 2008, while cedar was being cut on a regular basis, the loggers often counted up to 15 deer, busily browsing during daylight hours. Perhaps there were many more, living on the property, relishing the fresh cedar browse the loggers were providing. My hope was that the nutritional status of those deer would be high in the spring, more fawns would be born, and the racks on the bucks would be larger. Well, as already stated in Chapter 9, I only saw one buck during the 2009 season and it did not have a large rack but I did see many more deer than previous seasons.

It was interesting that the deer visiting the fallen cedars became comfortable with the loggers and almost as soon as a cedar tree was felled they would appear and begin browsing. One of the fellows even talked to them on a regular basis. But when I visited, which was about once per week for an hour or so, they recognized me as someone different and invariably they spooked away. Those browsing deer bedded down near those cedars every night and formed well-worn trails that were absolutely covered with deer droppings.

A summary of my hunting experience during the fall, '08, can be found in Chapt. 9, The Rifle.

This past winter, 2009, with much snow and cold, there were most certainly several deer residing on the property because every time I visited, with snowshoes or x-country skis, I chased up several deer. We received more snow than usual and the alfalfa in the neighboring fields was covered and flattened. Not surprisingly then, the tracks indicate that the deer were browsing and not too fussy as to what they are browsing on, including my newly planted hybrid aspen, white pine, and even domestic blueberries. Having all that excellent cedar browse last winter, perhaps it was a shock to them to have such slim pickings during this winter. The good news is that by the winter of 2010 and beyond, the clear-cut areas will have grown in and will provide considerably more browse.

Chapter Fourteen
Trespassing.

I admit to trespassing more than once, especially to get to some of my favorite fishing spots. But if land is posted, I do not feel right hunting there. This past deer hunting season I did trespass into posted land but I was tracking a wounded buck (see Chapter Nine). I fortunately was able to ask the land owner for permission to continue the tracking the next morning – I came upon his deer blind and he was occupying it. Unfortunately, I did not recover that buck. Some of my trespassing cases while fishing I write about in "Brook Trout and Uncle Willy" and they bring back many memories. I don't recall anyone trespassing into our farm property when I was a kid and trespassing was not a concern of my grandfather or uncles but I'm sure it happened. At least one of my buddies trapped mink on Long Crick, within our farm limits and without asking permission, even from me, but he did no damage. I recall he caught a mink one fall and was very happy. I happened to be with Cousin Ric one Sunday afternoon when he confronted a trespasser rumaging through their garage in broad daylight and he about scared the young man to death. Ric was really upset and made sure that young man would never again set foot on their farm and I would bet anything he didn't.

Now that I own acreage, especially with a brook trout crick meandering through it, I have become more sensitive to the possibility of trespassers and I have the land posted, mainly for legal/liability purposes. Shortly after we purchased the 40 acres I realized that people were trout fishing on my crick, the evidence being empty bait boxes and beer cans. Its a puzzle why fishermen and hunters litter. I confronted a lady picking morels one day in May. She claimed to have been given permission from the previous owner to enter the property and did not realize there was a new owner. I gave her permission to continue, not being a morel picker at the time. More recently I have been converted to finding those tasty morsels myself. A fellow stopped by one day in early December and asked if he could cut cedar branches for Christmas wreaths – I gave him permission but when I realized just how many cedar branches he was cutting – over $1000 worth, I stopped that. Typically, people will take advantage of you if you let them. But I will still allow any youngster to fish for brook trout. In fact I encourage it and have told everyone who lives nearby that the stream is open to youngsters for fishing.

Shortly after retirement I purchased a used semiautomatic 22 rifle with open sights for $75 from a local gun shop. It worked fine for the first few times I shot it but then it began to jam on a regular basis. I could never undo the jam out at my farm so I had to bring the rifle home to work on it. After the next jam I took it back to the gun shop I purchased it from. It cost me $35 and it worked fine for about 6 shots before it jammed again. I then took it to a different gun shop near our winter home, and what a shop that was! There were more guns than I could have counted. I swear the owner had every make and model ever manufactured and the store was so crowded with guns and hunting merchandise there were only narrow paths to move around. The man unfortunately was beaten up and robbed the year after I visited and he then closed the shop. That repair cost me $45. The repairs now had cost me as much as the rifle had. I brought the rifle back to our home up north and it worked for about 2 weeks before it jammed again.

After telling my brother-in-law Hank, a gun expert, my sob story, he volunteered to look at it. He would never say, "I will repair it," but only, "I will take a look at it." He took it apart and got it working fine, but that lasted only for one year. The next time it jammed I had had enough of that old 22 and decided to purchase a new one. Consulting with Hank led me to a new 22 semiautomatic rifle with a 10 shot clip and a telescopic sight. I asked Hank to join me at the firing range to "sight it in." After a few minor adjustments, we were hitting the bull's-eye at 50 yards almost every time and at 25 yards every time. I am saving that old 22 to be used as a single-shot target-shooting rifle by my grandsons.

I loved the way my new 22 handled and immediately became anxious to take it out to the farm and look for real game. It was December and the late deer bow season was open. Grouse season was also open but I had no intention of shooting a grouse on the ground now as a retiree, even though I bagged my first grouse while it was on the ground. Of course I knew there was no chance to bag one in the air with a 22, it being difficult enough with a shotgun. Besides, it would not be wise to shoot the 22 in the air with the houses and farms in the area. I drove out to the farm

Grouse, Deer, and Uncle Willy

on a cold day thinking I would cross-country ski and hunt at the same time. Rabbits and squirrels were going to be my game. There was about 6 inches of snow on the ground and the farm is flat enough so that I could do fine with one ski pole, holding the rifle in one hand and the ski pole in the other. My plan was to make a large circle just within the north edge, continuing along the east edge, and then come back along the road leading to my blind, more or less in the center of the property.

When I got to the north edge of the property I noticed a set of bootprints. Someone had come in from across the alfalfa field and through the barbed-wire fence. It surprised me as I had the property posted and the trespasser was so blatant. I was curious who this might be so I followed the tracks to the east low land, back toward and right up to my deer blind. I could see that the person had opened the door and looked inside, and then proceeded down to the crick. At that point I assumed the individual crossed the crick over the bridge and left the property going south. So I decided to stand under a tree and rest for a minute, all the while looking for squirrels and rabbits.

I was facing west and from the crick lowlands I spotted movement. The person was coming through the trees and did not see me until he was within 20 yards. I said,"Hey, how are you doing?" He stopped, looked surprised, and said, "OK." I could see he had a bow with an arrow at the ready and he had both hands in position ready to draw back the bow. It was a little disconcerting that he did not release his right hand from the bow string. I skied over toward him and then could see that he was just a youngster. I introduced myself as the owner of the property and asked him his name and age. "My name is Billy," he said, "and I'm

15 years old." He said he lived with his dad in the southern part of the state and was up for the weekend to bow hunt; he was staying with his mom. I told him he was hunting on private property and reminded him of the "No Hunting or Trespassing" signs posted along the periphery. He said his mom told him his uncle owned this land and it would be fine to hunt here. I asked who the uncle was and where his mother lived. He said the uncle was the dairy farmer to the southwest and that his mother lived up the road about a quarter mile north of my property, which is where he started from. I informed him that I owned this property, not his uncle, and that he should inform his mother of that. All this time the young man had both hands at the ready on his bow. That bothered me then and still bothers me to this day.

A trespasser. *As Jim stepped from under the tree, he waved to the young man trespassing on his 40 acres and asked, "How are you doing?" The young man said, "OK" but maintained his hand on his bow string, which was more than a little disconcerting to Jim. The young man, only 15, said his mother had given him permission and that she thought the land belonged to her brother, the dairy farmer. Jim offered to let the young man hunt for the remainder of the day but encouraged him to have his mother call him for permission to hunt. She didn't call and Jim never saw the young man again.*

I contemplated what to do and decided he was not doing any harm and that he might have a chance at a deer, which were abundant, or at least antlerless deer were, so I told him it would be OK if he hunted on my property for the remainder of the day. Then I said, "if you want to hunt tomorrow or thereafter, your mother will have to call me and ask permission." I told him my name but did not have a pencil to write down my phone number. Without thanking me he headed for the north edge of my 40 where he had entered. It was time for me to head home so I skied out to my truck which I had parked alongside the road and took my skis off. I noticed the young man walking up the road going north. I cased my 22, put my skis in my truck, and drove up to where he was walking. I had a pen in my truck so I wrote my name and phone number on a piece of a tissue box, passed it on to him, and suggested he have his mother call me to ask for permission to hunt. I would likely have allowed him to hunt and just wanted to make it clear to his mother that this was private land. She never called and I have not seen that young man since. Every once in awhile I think about him and wonder if he has found a different place to hunt and whether he has been successful. Then I am also reminded that he never took his hand off that bow string.

Through the years I have not had a problem with people trespassing on my property, with a few exceptions. One winter a snowmobiler snipped the barbed wire fence along the north edge, came right into my property, and proceeded to run over many of my newly planted pine trees. But I didn't see that individual. In a second case a fellow who occasionally worked at the neighboring dairy farm asked me if he could trap mink within my property. I gave him permission, not being a mink trapper myself. He set a mink trap just below where the crick crosses the road into my 40. The problem in this case was that mink trapping season had not yet opened. I found that out when talking to Reggie, the owner of the sporting goods store in our little town. Reggie got very upset as he knew the trapper's brother and had little regard for the whole family but he didn't call the DNR. Instead he called the trapper and gave him a piece of his mind. The trap was removed the next day. Coyote hunters with their dogs came barging through the property once but I saw no problem with that, their being hot on a trail. I came upon a man fishing for brook trout on the crick one summer, enjoying some success fishing in the "holes" I had worked hard to create. Now if a fisherman would use a barbless hook, return most of the smaller trout, perhaps keeping only a few above 8 inches for a fish fry, I wouldn't mind. But this fellow showed me a picture he took out of his wallet of 10 brook trout laid side by side. Then he dared to say, "I caught these all on the same day from this crick. Aren't they beauties?" He was smiling from ear to ear and obviously wanted my approval. I looked him right in the eye and answered very sternly, "Let me remind you that the daily limit is 5, that I have worked hard to improve this crick, and that I think you should be using a barbless hook and return everything you catch! Now I want you leave my property and I don't want to see you here ever again." Fortunately I haven't seen the fellow! Finally, this past turkey hunting season, spring, '09, I was walking along the north side of my 40 in the middle of the afternoon checking the alfalfa field to the north for turkeys when a man in camouflage came walking across the field. I was in camo too so he didn't see me. He blatantly came right to my property line, through the fence, and began walking into my property. I confronted him and all he said was, "I'm embarrassed." I suggested he note the

James Woodsing

private property signs and said my brother-in-law and I are both hunting within the 40, two probably being a sufficient number of hunters for 40 acres. I haven't seen him since.

Chapter Fifteen
Uncle Willy Reminisces

Like many youngsters, Uncle Willy began his hunting experiences with a BB gun. His father had no problem with Uncle Willy obtaining a BB gun but it was his mother who needed convincing. There were two things that made his mother say no. One was the safety concern in that she did not want him nor any of his friends to be hurt. The second was the cost. She asked, "How are you going to pay for it?" Knowing that her 12 yr old son did not have spending money she thought there was no chance he would obtain a BB gun. But Uncle Willy had a plan. "I will sell Cloverine Salve," he said. This salve was for chapped lips and chapped skin and was very necessary during those cold winters in the far north. "Well, you will have to sell a lot of salve," she said. Uncle Willy got all excited and sell salve he did, all through the farming community and to relatives and friends, until he had the money necessary for a Daisy BB gun and BBs. With the BB gun he learned the basics of shooting, the safety rules, and had much fun hunting squirrels, chipmunks, blackbirds, and even mice in the barn.

Uncle Willy learned a great deal about hunting from his older brother Ralph. When Ralph went grouse or deer hunting he would often let Uncle Willy tag along, even though Uncle Willy was not old enough to hunt legally and did not carry a rifle. Ralph was an easy-going, patient young man, and a good teacher. From Ralph he learned that grouse (partridge) can be most easily found in logged areas where an abundance of birch, aspen and evergreens are present for food and cover. He learned that deer like cedar swamps as they browse on the soft needles and ends of branches. Ralph showed him how to clean a grouse and how to field dress a deer. At this point Uncle Willy and I both remembered the characteristic odor when gutting a grouse. Neither of us could describe it but we clearly could recognize it even blindfolded. Finally, when he was 15, Uncle Willy and his 17 year old brother Ned obtained a single shot 22 rifle to share, purchased for them by their father, with which they became an expert shot. With this, their first rifle, Uncle Willy and Ned shot rabbits and grouse and did plenty of target shooting too.

I asked Uncle Willy if he remembered bagging his first buck. He remembered in great detail and related the story to me as follows. "When I was 18, I bought a big-game hunting license and bagged my first buck on the second day of the season. I was hunting with a 30-30, lever-action carbine bought for me by my brother Nate who was working in Detroit and making good money. My hunting companion was Gus, a neighbor. Gus had bagged his buck the first day of season in a forest owned by a local mining company so the two of us went back to the same area, which was high land called Happy Mountain, and we posted several hundred yards apart." Uncle Willy continued as if it was just yesterday but in fact it was 75 years ago. "There had been a thaw and then freezing temperatures returned putting a crust on the snow that would crunch when stepped through. It wasn't a very long time posting when I heard the crunch, crunch of someone or something walking towards me through the thicket. I thought it might be another hunter until I saw the large set of antlers. That nice buck was only 30 yards or so away from me. It stopped and looked right at me. Oh my, was I ever nervous. I had the shakes so badly it must have been buck fever. I didn't think I could even shoot but I did and I missed because I was shaking so badly. That buck jumped up and started running right past me and I kept shooting, shaking the whole time. I was determined to empty that rifle if I had to but on the 5th shot I hit it in the spine and it dropped only 5 yards from me. I was still very excited and decided to make sure it was dead so I was going to put a bullet through its head. Instead I hit one of the antlers, putting a nick in it. So I took one more shot and I finally hit it right in the head. That antler I nicked later broke off when we were dragging the deer out. After all these years, I still have that rack with the one half missing." Uncle Willy showed me that rack, which was nailed against the wall in his garage, and sure enough one half of the rack was missing. That half rack had 4 points.

 Gus had heard the shooting and later said to Uncle Willy, "Those shots were fired faster than I had ever heard shots fired and I thought it must have been a semi-automatic rifle." But it was Uncle Willy with that lever action carbine, adrenalin flowing freely, firing as fast as he could. Uncle Willy remembered that it was an 8 point buck but definitely a little on the thin side. They field dressed that deer and got it home to the farm that same day. The next day Uncle Willy skinned the buck and found two cartridges under the skin in the chest area, fairly close together, and cut them out. Later Uncle Willy's cousin John examined those cartridges and concluded that they were fired by different rifles. Apparently that buck had been shot previously, perhaps explaining its low weight, suffering from a wound inside the body. Uncle Willy and Gus dragged that buck almost 2 miles over tough terrain and finally ran out of light. The next day his father drove their Model T Ford as close as possible along a new logging road and they retrieved the buck. When Uncle Willy and his father processed that buck, they noted it was run down with hardly any fat and that the meat was "tough eating." They gave much of the meat to neighbors to avoid spoilage. There were no freezers then and electricity lines had not reached our farm yet anyway. That was quite a unique experience I thought and its no wonder Uncle Willy remembered all those details.

I then asked Uncle Willy if he usually got his buck in the following hunting seasons. He said, "Yes, I did, and the very next season father and I shot two bucks within minutes of each other." Uncle Willy never said, "my father," but only "father." He continued, "On the first few days of season we hunted at the hunting camp but the snow was so deep it was difficult to walk through the woods. So on the fifth day we hunted closer to home where the snow had settled and was not so deep. Even then there was the well-recognized phenomenon of 'lake effect' snow but there wasn't a name for it nor was there a precise weather forecast even on radio. TV was not invented yet and we didn't use our battery-operated radio very often. The farm had no electricity. Even the newspaper forecast was not very useful because the newspaper arrived a day late."

Uncle Willy went on to say, "Early in the afternoon we drove to an area near a tributary of Black Crick, called Spirit Crick. Father and I walked into an area of evergreens where we thought deer might be feeding on cedar browse. I had some mink traps set along Black Crick so I told father that I wanted to check my traps but I had to cross the crick at a shallow spot, a riffle, to get to the traps. Father decided to join me and after crossing the crick, we quietly walked over a rise. There among a batch of aspen, balsam, and spruce was a large deer with a thick neck, an indication of a buck in rut. We both looked carefully and thought there were antlers so father told me to go ahead and shoot." Uncle Willy continued with the story somewhat animated now. "My first shot went right through the heart and the buck dropped on the spot. Before we could walk toward that deer, another deer appeared and this time the antlers were very clearly visible. Father shot this second deer, it also being only 25 yards away, and it dropped after only two leaps. Those two bucks were probably chasing after the same doe. We field dressed both deer, mine being an 8 pointer and father's a 6 pointer. We tagged them and identified the spot so we could find the deer when we returned. It was a long distance from father's Model T Ford and by now it was getting late. So, instead of dragging those two large bucks out that evening, we headed home. The next day we hitched up our team of horses to a low sled with a flat bottom but no runners, called a stone boat because it was used to pick stones (rocks) from the farm fields. When we came to Spirit Crick, those horses would not cross that crick, try as I might to command them to do so. So father took the reins and succeeded in getting them to wade through pulling that stone boat along through the water. Father must have had a more commanding tone of voice. Well, it took the better part of the day to get to those deer, load them on the sled, and get them back home." Uncle Willy remembered one of the horses was a female named Mary but he could not remember the other one. I asked if it was Chubby, a horse I remembered as a youth, but he said it was probably Shorty and that Chubby came later. Uncle Willy remembered those deer having very strong tasting meat. He called them "swamp bucks."

Grouse, Deer, and Uncle Willy

Father and son bagged two bucks within a few minutes of each other. *No sooner had Uncle Willy shot one nice buck but another nice buck appeared. His father shot that one.*

Another interesting buck kill by Uncle Willy occurred on the first day of season, Nov. 15, 1954. He related the story to me as follows: "I had come to the farm from California for a vacation to deer hunt. On November 14th, the day before the season opened, I joined a friend, Harvey, at his hunting cabin just south of Black Crick, and we got ready to hunt the next day, opening day. It was very warm for Nov. 15. Harvey headed south and I headed north towards Black Crick. After a few hrs of not seeing anything, I walked to sister Myrna's house which was only a mile away and hunted there and along the way during mid-day hrs. Again I saw nothing so I stopped to visit with Myrna for awhile and had coffee and one of her delicious home-made biscuits, then I headed back to Harvey's camp. Harvey had bagged an 8 pointer which he already had hanging from the buck pole in front of the camp. It was too late to go back out hunting by then so we cooked some of the liver for dinner but we over-cooked it." Uncle Willy made a face and continued. "That liver was so strong tasting I could hardly eat it. The next morning because it was so warm the guys brought Harvey's buck to the farm, skinned and processed it and refrigerated the meat. By 1954 we had electricity and a refrigerator. I told Harvey I wanted to hurry back to his camp so I could get out hunting before dark. When arriving at the camp, I went north again and climbed up on a cedar windfall and got comfortably positioned, facing north. I was hunting with an 8 mm German Mauser I had purchased from an old-timer in San Pedro, California, who worked for Douglas Aircraft with me. It was an excellent rifle with a perfect barrel. I put a peep sight on it. I should have never sold that rifle. Anyway, after a few minutes I heard a deer blow behind me so I turned slowly and quietly and saw a huge buck with a big rack. I was in an awkward position and I was going to shoot from my left side but as the buck approached I switched to my right side to shoot. The buck ran toward me and turned about 40 feet away so I swung my rifle around and shot again but the buck kept running with its butt end toward me and its white tail high. I aimed right into the middle of the rump and fired. The buck took a few leaps and I heard crashing noises. With that shot I had broken its rump bone. I quickly ran to the deer and finished it off with a head shot and field dressed it. I then went back to camp and brother Ralph was there so the two of us went back to the deer. Examining the deer showed that the first shot had gone rather cleanly

Grouse, Deer, and Uncle Willy

through the chest, not causing much damage." Uncle Willy continued, "if I had not got that lucky shot into its rump bone, that buck would likely not have been found because there was no snow and it was heading for a thick swamp. I then borrowed my brother-in-law's Model A Farmall tractor and we hauled that buck out. It was a 10 pointer that weighed 215 lbs. It was good eating meat and I brought some back to California on ice." Uncle Willy added, "But to this day I regret giving the antlers to Harvey. I have a picture of that big buck I will show you." And he did show me the picture and indeed it was a monster buck. What a great way to spend vacation time and what a story to bring back to tell his co-workers in California.

A few weeks before the 2008 deer season opened, I talked to Uncle Willy by phone. Of course we related stories about hunting and fishing. He happened to be preparing Lake Superior lake trout for his dinner, still living alone at 92 years old. He said his neighbor had caught several trout from the "big lake" which is how he referred to Lake Superior, and had kindly given him one. Toward the end of our conversation I asked him if he was going to hunt deer. "I don't know," he said, "my legs are not good. Maybe I could hunt from the door of Nephew Art's hunting cabin." I encouraged him to do that and wished him luck. But he did not hunt and it is likely his hunting days are over. But he still has some hunting stories to tell and when he reads this book his memory will be triggered for plenty more. And what experiences he has had. He is a special man, a special uncle, and a special hunting companion.

About the Author

James M. Woodsing, an internationally published author, grew up on a small dairy farm in the north woods. In the absence of a father, who had died in an accident when he was an infant, Woodsing was fortunate to have his Uncle Willy as an outdoors companion and role model. Uncle Willy had the interest, patience, and enthusiasm to teach the young Woodsing about the outdoors, especially about grouse and deer. Woodsing was thus introduced to hunting as a twelve yr old and subsequently enjoyed many hunting adventures with his uncle during which his love for grouse and deer grew. He did not miss a hunting season until he began his career, when he took a long respite. In retirement, he has returned to the sport he always loved. Woodsing recalls his early hunting experiences and vividly narrates them in a unique style with rich and realistic illustrations. Personality differences, Woodsing being impatient while the Uncle is laid back, add an interesting aspect to their close bond. Woodsing clearly treasures his youth and presents a captivating recollection of a young boy developing a strong love for hunting grouse and deer and an even stronger love for his uncle.

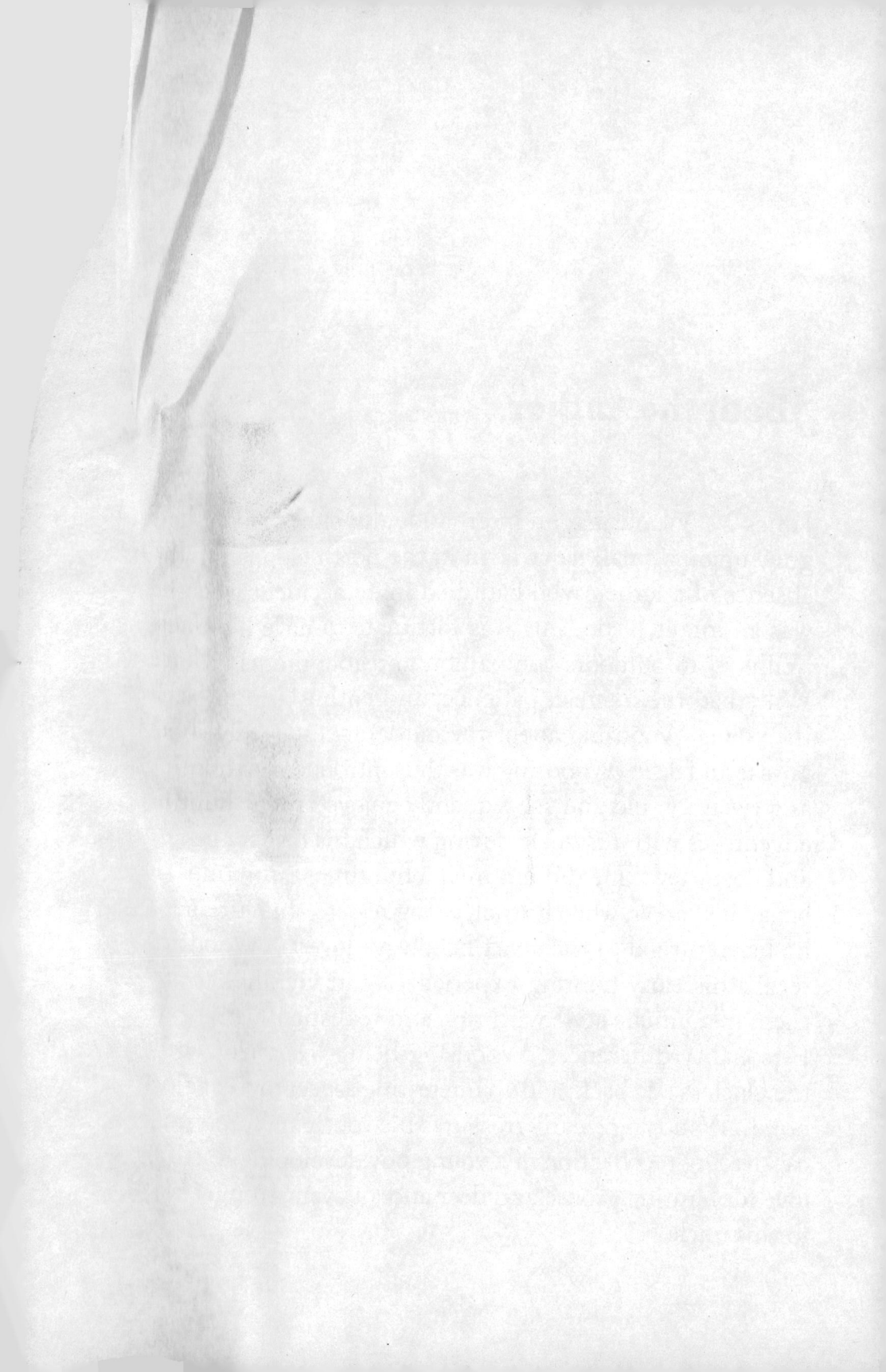